CLIENTS COME LAST

CLIENTS COME LAST

VOLUNTEERS
AND
WELFARE
ORGANIZATIONS

ESTHER STANTON

With an introduction
by AMITAI ETZIONI

SAGE PUBLICATIONS
Beverly Hills, California

For information address:

 **SAGE PUBLICATIONS, INC.**
275 South Beverly Drive
Beverly Hills, California 90212

First Printing

Printed in the United States of America

Standard Book Number 8039-0063-5

Library of Congress Catalog Card No. 71-103484

Designed by HANFT/LAGARDERE/HOFFMAN

Composition by WESTYPE

"Yet the image was just that: an image. They even called it that and never noticed what they'd said. The reality differed."

—Philip Wylie

ACKNOWLEDGEMENTS

It would be difficult for me and perhaps embarrassing for them if I were to attempt to credit those people of "Pangloss" who have helped make this book possible. I can, however, with much delight, acknowledge my great indebtedness to Professor Alfred Lindesmith for the encouragement, guidance, and help which he so generously gave from the very beginning to the very end. For stimulating criticism and thoughtful suggestions, I wish also to thank Professors Richard H. Hall, Austin Turk, and James Wood. And finally, I am not only grateful for Professor Etzioni's interest—I am also hopeful because he shares this concern.

—E.S.

CONTENTS

1 IMAGE MANIPULATION | 19 |

The Play is the Thing. The Dramatization of Virtue. The Division of Labor. The Medium and the Message. The Agency and Its Image. The Pressure to be Rational. Ethical Misrepresentation. Framework of Analysis. The Dramaturgical Perspective.

2 THE COMMUNITY CONTEXT | 35 |

The Subject. The Agency and Its Activities. Professed Goals and Agency Programs. Previous Research. Historical Background. Philosophical Split.

3 DEFINITIONAL DISCREPANCIES | 47 |

Stigma. Semantic Maneuvers. THE COOLING PROCESS. Heating Up the Definition. Diversionary Action.

4 THE FACADE OF FORMAL ORGANIZATION 61 |

FORMAL ORGANIZATION. Organization of Staff. The Irrational Aspects of Rational Organization. Operationalizing the Formal Organization. The Informal Organization.

5 THE CASTING OF CIVIC DRAMA | 73 |

VOLUNTEER TYPOLOGIES. The Pariahs. The Career Volunteers. Good Works Volunteers. The Loners. Overlapping Categories. STAFF TYPOLOGY. RE-CRUITMENT OF STAFF. The True Believer. SINCERE RECRUIT TO DEDICATED CYNIC.

FOREWORD

This book speaks directly to one of the most disconcerting phenomena of our time: the elaborate and encompassing attempts to cover social realities with elaborate facades which make society seem more appealing, humane, and participatory than it really is. While the study dismantles the facade of only one institution, unveiling its true nature and, at the same time, exploring the ways in which its facades are manufactured, it addresses those engaged in all such endeavors as well as those walled in by them.

Societal duplicity—the deliberate and unwitting separation of societal images from the underlying reality—is a much more all-encompassing phenomenon than the yarns of advertising, the fallacies of public relations, and the hollow promises of politicians. What has been called into question is the American way of life and the American dream—the promise of equality, affluence and freedom for all—as poverty, racism and war remain the constant and intimate companions of that promise. There is the deepening division between the claims of a democratic system and the limitations both of those who can be elected, and of those who can vote. One has only to examine the disenfranchisement of Negroes in the South and of youth between the ages of eighteen and twenty-one together with the continuous evasion of the one man, one vote rule, to see how the system deviates from the democratic posture.

The hollowness of these facades is evident in the national entertainment, television's wasteland, and in materialistic way of life made up of status races contested with consumer goods. Such leisure and consumption fail to provide true satisfaction and involvement, and must be paid for by jobs which are not meaningful. Thus, like the patients and volunteers in the agency studied here, the average citizen moves through a life that is as artificial, colorless, and pliable as a cellophane wrapper. Only occasionally, recently more frequently, do the unmobilized urges break through.

The erection of facades is hardly a novel phenomen. There have always been political formulae, myths, and efforts, conscious and unconscious, that mask social reality to enhance its acceptability to those who benefit less from its existing structures than those at the top. What previous work suggests, and Esther Stanton's study helps to ramify, is that we are now entering a historical phase in which inauthenticity, the generic term we use to refer to all dissimulation, is increasing in scope, complexity, and intricacy. (A review of such previous work can be found in Chapter 21 of *The Active Society* [Etzioni, 1968].) This proliferation is due in part to greater mass involvement in sociopolitical life. It is too expensive to keep the masses at bay and at work by use of force or pay-offs. Public relations, or indoctrination (in totalitarian societies), is the cheapest means of control. In addition, the means of manipulation have multiplied with the evolution of empirical social science and with the development of more potent means of mass communication (45,000,000 television sets in the United States and media-hogging communication satellites).

The psychological effect on the citizen of the mounting efforts to manipulate him is not the now traditional sense of being alienated, of being excluded; such feelings can be mobilized into opposition. The new world of distorting mirrors results in deep existential restlessness, leading to withdrawal as with the use of tranquilizers and narcotics, to reliance on psychotherapy and manufactured groups to escape loneliness, illustrated in this book both by the patients and the staff, and high incidences of other forms of neurotic conduct from alcoholism to suicide. The basic reason that inauthenticity does not cause the individual to feel locked out is that those who find themselves manipulated find that they did share in the process; they assisted the hand that played with their selves by vigorously pursuing material objects and empty jobs in spite of an inner sense of the false quality of their projects, their public lives, and their assumed selves.

The author is most incisive in describing and analyzing the forms that facade fabrication assumes and the ways in which facades are hammered together. She offers no prescription as to how a person caught in such a condition may free himself, how he can pierce the walls and, having seen the light, expand the opening, joining other inmates in building a world more responsive to their basic needs.

However, in those matters that she does attend to, Stanton is forthright and forceful in analysis and style. She does not seek to spare her subject or her readers, nor does she lose her insight by fragmenting the perspective she has gained into countless specialized details. She has thus written a book which moves, occasionally shocks, and surpasses in its own authenticity many others on any reader's shelf.

—Amitai Etzioni

Center for Policy Research
New York and Washington, D.C.
October, 1969

PREFACE

This is a study of the dramatization of virtue. It is concerned with the civic drama—the modern morality play which is enacted daily in a wide variety of secular settings for the purpose of persuading people to undertake those tasks which are called humanitarian. Much of it is built upon the dramaturgical framework proposed by Erving Goffman in *The Presentation of Self in Everyday Life* (1954). My purpose is to describe both the techniques and consequences of the public relations effects and performance routines by which a private philanthropic social agency attempts to fabricate an image acceptable to its environment.

The study arises out of the deep conviction that voluntary social action, cooperatively undertaken, is the essence of community. Within the book, I shall attempt to show that the delegation of concern entails a misapplication of rational principles to what is essentially a nonrational area of human behavior; as a result, honest, decent, and idealistic people—both paid staff and volunteers—subvert their own humanitarianism in activities which are mutually manipulative.

My husband, who is sometimes distressingly perceptive, has suggested that a more appropriate title might be "Confessions of a People Helper." I suspect he is right. Certainly the events and behaviors which I am about to describe were accomplished through the collusion of those of us who were participants. My only defense is that at the time—at least part of the time—it seemed like a good idea.

I think it is important to mention here that this was not initially conceived as a study in the sociology of corruption. At the outset, I was interested in identifying and describing certain dramatic communicative techniques which I believed to be influential in the outcomes of a mental health association's attempt to combat stigma and enlist public support. However, I discovered early that what is communicated is often less important than what is concealed. Moreover, I discovered that the cooperative efforts required for the management of information have unintended consequences.

The serendipity pattern—the unexpected and anomalous finding—is an exciting, but not necessarily painless experience. In this case, my data not only discredit much of my own work in the field of mental health, but may also devalue the efforts of people who were my friends. A community services council associate, with many years experience, read the manuscript and observed: "You are unfair to Mental Health. What you have written is true, but there are many other agencies much worse."

The point, I think, is well taken. A scale of "worst" to "best" is irrelevant, but the judgment indicates that the behaviors which I shall describe are observable in a greater or lesser degree throughout the entire system of community supported agencies.

Methodology and Source of Data

The study claims no methodological innovations. Inasmuch as publicity and performances are devices to control information, participant observation is probably the only means by which a researcher can become privy to the backstage secrets and mechanics of the civic drama which are shared by the key performers.

I would like to think that the research procedure approximates that which S.T. Bruyn (1966) has described as "The New Empiricism" —a methodology employed by both the participant observer and the phenomenologist. In discussing the role of the researcher, Bruyn says:

> He approaches his subject making every effort to eliminate the preconceptions he has about the nature of the subject under investigation. He must have no hypothesis to direct him; he takes special pains to conduct his research with a totally open mind, open in depth to all the stimuli that impinge upon his consciousness during his investigation.

In my case, achieving openmindedness presented no problems: the mind involved in the collection of data was completely unencumbered by any systematized body of sociological knowledge which might have created inhibiting preconceptions. The situation was a reversal of the conventional course of events: it was the research problem which stimulated the interest in sociology, rather than vice versa.

Less than a year before the collection of data began, I accepted a six weeks' assignment, as a freelance journalist, to handle publicity for a private social agency in a middle-sized metropolitan center; and at the end of the assignment, joined the agency as a fulltime "professional" staff member with responsibilities for publicity and volunteer programs. During the first six months of employment, discrepancies between what was and what was professed became a source of increasing interest. For example, why did the agency overtly profess to be concerned for the welfare of mental patients, yet covertly protect a hospital in a situation where patients' rights were violated? Why was the volunteer overtly praised as the *sine qua non*, yet covertly regarded as an agent who could not be trusted to act in the interests of the organization unless carefully supervised?

The attempt to find answers to these and other questions led to the enrollment in a sociology course that autumn, and it was during this first class that the role of participant observer crystallized. For the next two years, with the ultimate objective of using the experience as the basis of a study, I observed, questioned, and kept careful notes. In graduate school and the study of Goffman, I found the necessary theoretical framework and conceptual tools. (It will be obvious that I am more than a pallid admirer of Goffman.)

Sometime later, when I became a fulltime student, the role of participant was dropped, but the scope of the observation was enlarged to include the activities of other organizations which utilized volunteers. Thus, although this study primarily deals with the social world of an agency staff as it is subjectively experienced, the observations are based on a number of associations.

As Bruyn points out, in either the phenomenological or the participant observer approach, there are dangers of bias and subjectivity:

> In the process of taking their role, he becomes personally involved in living with the culture he studies. He then has the problem of balancing his involvement with objective detachment in arriving at an accurate accounting of the culture [Bruyn, 1966].

Well aware of the dangers of bias, as well as those of memory distortion, I took advantage of an opportunity to update and verify earlier research data and impressions by returning to the original agency in a peripheral role during the final compilation of data and the writing of much of this book. I thought it interesting that the inaccuracies I discovered were consistently in the direction of understatement.

The chief sources of data are observation, interviews, conversations, and official documents. Although informal interviews rather than interview schedules were used, quotations are as nearly as possible verbatim. Interviews were conducted on a highly selective and broadly representative basis from all levels of agency activity, from staff and volunteers—including the disenchanted as well as the enthusiastic—and from staff members of cooperating organizations in both subordinate and superordinate relationships.

Methodologically, I shall attempt to formulate some broad general propositions which will need further empirical verification in comparative study.

1
IMAGE MANIPULATION

There appears to be consensus among the observers of American society that the crux of the problem—almost any problem—is to find some means of motivating citizens to take seriously their responsibilities for democratic participation.

Perhaps the important issue is not how can citizens be motivated, but rather, how can they take seriously participation which is increasingly an illusion?

The paradox of the situation lies in the fact that although there is a surplus of social problems, there is a dearth of opportunity for *effective* action through traditional channels. The average citizen, in the event that he is moved to make a contribution to his community, ordinarily opts for established associations. However, if his qualifications survive the screening process, and if his enthusiasm outlasts the orientation sessions, he often finds that his humanitarian impulse is severely strained by the expediencies of organized altruism. Instead of experiencing meaningful involvement, he is *provided* "a sense of participation."

This curious phrase is so frequently used by the planners of social action that it deserves careful examination. If the sense of participation is something which can be provided—something to be passively accepted rather than actively experienced—the reality of the participant role becomes questionable.

What does the expression mean? Does it imply that the layman has come to be considered an unreliable anachronism in a world of professional problem solvers? Does it indicate that the function of a volunteer is to perpetuate a myth of voluntarism? And if the citizen's role is to sustain an illusion, what is the function of the expert who directs his efforts? If both are involved in a charade, what are the consequences for organizational goals?

Is it also possible to provide the victim of the problem "a sense of being helped?"

The answers to these questions are not self evident. The simulations and subterfuges which clothe social action are so convincingly rationalized under the rubric "good public relations" that it is difficult to distinguish what seems to be from what is. The difficulty is compounded for those who are actively involved. The immediacy of their day to day problems is far more compelling than philosophical examinations of the nature of reality. Moreover, if the citizen—or for that matter, the professional—becomes disenchanted with the under-achievement of kick-off luncheons, committee meetings, planning sessions, and award ceremonies, it is he who is discredited. He has failed his "sincerity test" in commitment to his community.

Such loss of commitment is rarely publicly expressed. When illusions are societally prescribed and celebrated, and when reality is perceived dimly or not at all, the individual may feel somehow cheated by pseudo participation, but his discontent is tinged with guilt. If he is able to articulate his disenchantment, he may lend his voice to those who accuse our institutions of irrelevancy. But more often than not, if there is a response to his charge, it is directed to improving the institutional image rather than to repairing the institutional flaws.

If traditional associations are unresponsive, what of those which are new? Can the citizen become more meaningfully involved in ventures which are relatively young? Perhaps initially, but for the most part, those who are attempting to construct new institutions appear unable to break the fetters of the old. Patterns of behavior which have brought success in the past are not easily relinquished—not even when such behaviors are irrelevant to present problems. Thus, the innovation is "modified" to fit the familiar formula. And when the patterns of relationships remain the same, the end result can be little more than a new front on an old structure.

The purpose of this book is to attempt to separate the illusions from the realities of community action. As an examination of image manipulation in social welfare, it is a study of the rules, roles, and relationships which emerge in the bureaucratization of philanthropy and the delegation of concern. Because it is written from the vantage point of the involved participant observer, it is not only concerned with the causes of citizen frustration, but also with the consequences experienced by the professionals who maintain the participatory facade.

It is not an attempt to identify villains. The behaviors with which we shall be concerned are often manipulatory, ingratiating, and designed to deceive. But the people are decent, well meaning, community-minded individuals, trapped in a system which they themselves perpetuate.

The Play is the Thing

Essentially, the central problem in the mobilization for action stems from the fact that many of our conventional philanthropic associations have become the producers of a kind of modern morality play—a civic drama—in which community leaders and would-be leaders are provided a context for the presentation of a well publicized altruistic self. In their starring roles, these actors become identified as protagonists of the worthy cause. Their performances are staged before cooperative audiences; the dramatic effect is intensified by the backstage machinations of a staff of paid technicians.

Alexis de Tocqueville, without whom no discussion of American society can be complete, more than a century ago warned: "If men are to remain civilized, or become so, the art of associating together must grow and improve. . ." (De Tocqueville, 1862: II, Bk.2; Chap. 5). The vast number of voluntary associations in existence today would seem to indicate that we have heeded de Tocqueville's warning. However, I am suggesting that the skills we have developed are organizational—not associational. The delegation of concern imposes rational principles on a nonrational area of human behavior. And the preoccupation with public relations transforms the *art* of associating together into the *art form* of civic drama.

If the theatrics are not openly recognized as such, it is because the make-believe roles are a very real part of the normative pattern of the social milieu. The civic drama has evolved as a means of capturing the imagination of the public and winning its support. It is based on the assumption that if a worthy cause is made visible and vivid, and if it is publicly supported by influential citizens, the rank and file will be motivated to emulate the altruistic efforts of their betters.

The Dramatization of Virtue

Sociologists have devoted considerable attention to the dramatization of evil (Tannenbaum, 1938: 17-21)—that process by which a society identifies, labels, shames and excludes those individuals whom it considers morally unacceptable. But the other side of the coin has consequences equally worthy of serious consideration. If a society makes public examples of its villains, it will also need models of that behavior which is considered exemplary. And when none are available, they will have to be invented.

At the national level, the investing of modern mortals with mythic proportions has become a public relations speciality which has been documented by historians and journalists. However, there must also be heroes of the middle range—people who, at the community level, can demonstrate the desirable deviance of supercitizenry.

In earlier times, candidates for these roles were provided by the church; but since a secular society demands secular heroes the action has moved to the community arena. Nowadays, the antithesis of the evildoer is the do-gooder. Because heroism demands sacrificial effort, it is preferable that he be an amateur. Because a role model requires optimum visibility, it is necessary that he be publicly exhibited.

Whether the publicized performer of the altruistic act is a theatrically skilled pretender or a bona fide activist is often not so much of a matter of sincere commitment as of available time. In either event, the part-time hero does not have to be a self-made hero. He can be created in the imagery of social welfare, his impeccable performance assured by the professional ministrations of the agency staff.

The Division of Labor

The private philanthropic social agency, representing the community's principal voluntary effort to cope with social problems, is a major vehicle for this process. Nongovernmental, it has frequently been established as a formalization of a citizens' movement for or against something societally perceived as good or evil. Although it commands a large share of the charity dollar and plays an important role in community decision making, it is an area of sociological research which contains many voids.

Philip Selznick's description (1943) of the typical voluntary association as "manned by a small core of individuals . . . around whom there fluctuates a loosely bound mass of dues payers," has a limited application to today's metropolitan social agency. Image conscious, grant wise, and career oriented—professionalized at both staff and volunteer levels—the private agency has become a sophisticated bureaucratic organization whose dues payers have been superseded by the United Fund Allocations Committee. Its board and committee members are practiced in the arts of volunteersmanship, men and women selectively recruited from business and professional strata.

Because the formalization of health and welfare associations is so often viewed as "progress," few authors in the social service field are able to resist the invidious comparison of the modern social worker to the much maligned Lady Bountiful. While it is true that Lady B. operated without theoretical orientation, it is not at all evident that the expertise of her present-day replacement has produced the promised panacea. In fact, it might even be argued that rather than offering a solution, the private agency has become a part of the problem.

David Riesman (1954: 232) has described the professionals of such organizations as "the full time planners of other peoples' short-time bursts of energy and masochism." The wit of Riesmans's apt description diverts attention from its truth. The professional social activator is trained in a helping discipline which has high ethical standards. But in the institutionalization of altruism, Lady Bountiful's husband becomes Chairman of the Board, sentimentalism is replaced by "sound business practices," and the pragmatic approach channels the proficiency of the expert to that which is expedient rather than to that for which he was trained. He is no sadist—in fact, his capacity for masochistic behavior may exceed that of the volunteer. However dedicated, he must help sustain the imagery of civic drama. And the division of labor required by this activity creates an uncertain alliance in which both amateurs and professionals play discrepant roles.

To understand the process by which all of this comes about requires a step by step analysis. Therefore, we must backtrack a bit, define our terms, and attempt to situate the problem within a concrete community context.

The Medium and the Message

As a species of voluntary association, the philanthropic health and welfare agency is a medium. Its manifest function is to transmit information concerning the desirability of certain action in order to influence nonassociational persons to cooperate in the implementation of the action. People oriented rather than profit oriented, the agency is dependent upon private contributions which it may receive directly from individuals and groups and/or indirectly as an allocation from a mass-fund-raising organization.

Essentially there are two types of unified-fund-supported agencies: (1) organizations for maintaining the status quo, and (2) organizations for bringing about social change (Babchuk and Edwards, 1965). In the first and largest group, the emphasis is placed on filling inherent needs by providing aid and services as ongoing community institutions.

That the need for aid and services may be structurally determined is not the primary concern of the status quo agency. It directs its efforts to those individuals who, according to Erving Goffman (1952) have experienced "the disappointment of reasonable expectations as well as misguided ones" and are therefore both troubled and troublesome in a success-oriented society. In effect, it functions to "cool out society's marks. . .to pacify and reorient the disorganized person. . .to send the patient back in a condition in which he can no longer cause trouble to others or can no longer make a fuss." Included here are such organizations as Family Service, Children's Bureau, Red Cross, and Travelers' Aid.

Agencies of the second category—those dedicated to changing society—provide aid and services only as stopgap measures or demonstration projects; their principal objective is the elimination of specific social problems through education, legislation, research, and improved treatment. Among others, this classification would include the health organizations, Planned Parenthood, civil rights and anti-poverty groups.

To be effective, agencies of the first category must survive. In the second category, to be effective is to eliminate the need for survival.

The Agency and Its Image

The high survival rate of social change agencies is not necessarily evidence of failure; however, it does suggest that if the organization is not effectively moving toward its goals, it is *effectively conveying the impression of effectiveness*. It is probable that the truth lies somewhere in between: few organizations are completely ineffective; most organizations attempt to enhance their images by presenting an idealized version of their activities.

In business, enhancing the corporate image is a public relations process designed to manipulate the demand structure of the environment. However, since business is dependent upon profit, the practice has a built-in limitation. An attractive "package" may seduce the impulsive buyer, but consumer loyalty is ultimately determined by package content. An enhanced image may help create and maintain the demand, but it cannot, of itself, fill the demand. At some point the organization must deliver a product or service whose acceptance or rejection is translated into profit or loss. Thus, the balance sheet provides the feedback which impels the system to make the necessary corrections.

The organization dealing with the intangibles of social improvement is not constrained by this limitation. In the absence of profit, it has no concrete evaluative feedback. Activities (i.e., "services") can be quantified, but qualitative evaluation is very difficult. Still more important, *the buyer and the consumer are not the same person.* The individual who supports the agency is frequently far removed from the individual who needs or gets the agency service. If the donor has delegated his dollar allocation to the United Fund, he is twice removed. Therefore, whether the unknown welfare recipient gets something for nothing or nothing for nothing is information for which no direct channels of communication are provided.

The situation presents a sizeable problem: to achieve its professed goals, the agency must serve the consumer; but to survive, it need only please the donor. Theoretically therefore, by controlling negative feedback, the organization can substitute packaging for product. With the elimination of constraints, image manipulation may be substituted for goal-directed action.

The Pressure to be Rational

If the neutralization of constraints enables an organization to sustain a deceptive facade, it does not necessarily follow that strict accountability will make an organization effective. As a matter of fact, in community-funded associations, the pressure to be rational is in itself a goal-distorting mechanism. The boards of laymen who control private agencies bring to this part time activity the pervasive bias that businesslike organization is desirable for every organizational enterprise. Thus, the private association is continuously constrained to make its operation efficient.

In *Modern Organizations*, Amitai Etzioni (1964: 8-9) points out that efficiency and effectiveness do not always go hand in hand. He suggests:

> Measuring effectiveness and efficiency raises several thorny problems. When an organization has a goal which is limited and concrete, it is comparatively easy to measure effectiveness. . .however, when we come to organizations whose output is not material. . . , statements about effectiveness are extremely difficult to validate.
>
> Most organizations under pressure to be rational are eager to measure their efficiency. Curiously, the very effort. . .often has quite undesired effects from the point of view of organizational goals. Frequent measuring tends to encourage the overproduction of highly measurable items and neglect of the less measurable ones.

The emphasis on quantification, whatever its source, is the hobgoblin which plagues clergy, social workers, teachers—in fact, almost anyone who is organizationally involved in a helping profession subject to lay control. The pressure to be rational, which is exerted through the granting or withholding of rewards, cannot be ignored if the organization is to survive. However, when the association concerned with human problems is forced to make efficiency more important than effectiveness, not only will there be neglect of less measurable activities, it is also almost inevitable that democratic process will be replaced by bureaucratic process, public education will be replaced by public relations, and image manipulation will displace goal-directed action.

The strain toward the production of quantifiable results underlies much of the public relations effort. Decibels, figuratively speaking, provide a highly acceptable substitute for concrete measurable units. The organization which "speaks with the loudest voice" or which most vigorously "blows its own horn" surrounds itself with an aura of newsworthiness. In the public mind, the quantity of favorable publicity is assumed to be directly correlated to the quality of good produced. Thus, the greater the amount of recognition in mass media, the more credible is the image of organizational effectiveness.

Ethical Misrepresentation

Image manipulation has become not so much an organizational choice as an organizational imperative. Inasmuch as it is a public relations axiom that such activity is an efficient means of implementing organizational goals, the association which overlooks this shortcut is considered remiss—if not downright negligent. If the image does not reflect the underlying reality, if it is an illusion, the deceptions and manipulations required to sustain the illusion are predicated on rational principles. Moral values may prescribe honest representation, but social mores condone ethical misrepresentation. In other words, although it is believed that the self or the organization ought to be what it represents itself to be, the exaggerated claims of the manipulated image are accepted as rational self-interest so long as the deceptive aspects are not perceived as societally disadvantageous.

To argue with this public relations tenet is to be considered unrealistic. To pose a model of an absolutely sincere society is to strip away those niceties of civilization which make life bearable and interaction possible. I would agree that such a model is impractical—much of the reality from which we are protected is irrelevant, distracting, distasteful, or merely tedious. However, if communication is essential to the integrity of a society, and if image manipulation involves the distortion of communicated information, the social costs of such behavior need to be reckoned.

Framework of Analysis

Because so much of the terminology connected with imagery emphasizes the reality of the illusion rather than the illusions of reality, if we are to make an accounting we must first clarify the concept. An image is not a prefabricated entity waiting to be perceived. The so-called image projector is merely a supplier of materials—communications—which become the basis for a mental construct which is assembled and completed in one fashion or another in the imagination of the perceiver.

The preoccupation with projecting a desirable image has replaced an earlier concern for protecting a valued reputation. The differences, while subtle, are important. Reputation is a product of *concrete information* (whether true or false) most commonly communicated in face-to-face interaction. An image, on the other hand, is essentially a bundle of *ambiguous impressions*—fragmented information—impersonally communicated, selectively perceived, and subjectively evaluated. Whereas good repute was maintained by the avoidance of action which was, or appeared to be, evil (i.e., discreditable), a desirable image can be contrived by the dramatization of activities which are, or appear to be, creditable. This distinction is crucial. The management of impressions (with the use of public relations techniques) does not require that discreditable activities be avoided, only that they be concealed.

In *The Presentation of Self in Everyday Life,* Goffman describes impression management as a largely nonverbal, presumably unintentional type of communication in which an individual, in interaction, either consciously or unconsciously utilizes devices ordinarily associated with theatre—setting, props, costuming, manner, etc.—to stage a "performance" designed to convince an audience that the impressions he is fostering are faithful representations of the underlying reality. He suggests that the actor's purpose in such a performance is

> To control the conduct of others, especially their responsive treatment of him, by influencing the definition of the situation which others come to formulate. . .by expressing himself in such a way as to give them the kind of impression that will lead them to act voluntarily in accordance with his plans [Goffman, 1959: 4-5].

Image manipulation is impression management *sans* innocence. Designed to impress a public rather than a private audience, it is professionalized, institutionalized, and extended to verbal definitions of the situation which are communicated by mass or other media and may be quite apart from the dramatic interaction.

Because for many people, these verbal definitions—the publicity—are the introductory and sometimes only source of relevant information, this is an essential communication. For the organization it has a dramaturgical significance because it becomes, in an important sense, the *scenario* which determines much of the subsequent behavior.

It should also be noted that like the performance, the dramatic impact of the publicity is more often a consequence of context than of content. The graphic verbal description can conjure up potent imagery; however, inferences are drawn not just from the message, but also from the medium. The front page, prime time television, and the sleek brochure are, in themselves, informative. A message becomes impressive when it is impressively conveyed.

When the initial definitive claims are presented in an impressive context, and when their content becomes a matter of public record, the performance will be locked in to the verbal definition. Thus, the sustaining of an organizational image is complex.

In contrast to the interaction-limited presentation of self, the presentation of a collectivity is rigorously proscribed by its advance publicity. The solo performer in everyday life, if he is sensitive to the response of his audience and if he has not overstated his claims, can continuously and advantageously adjust, modify, or redefine his situation as necessity indicates. But to sustain a collective definition of the situation requires the intimate cooperation of individual actors in team performances (Goffman, 1959: 75-105) where spontaneous adjustment, modification, or redefinition by any one participant can jeopardize the effective participation of his teammates. And finally, as Goffman (1959: 93-105) notes, to the extent that there must be advance agreement on any misrepresentation of reality, teammates will be in collusion in the sharing of "guilty knowledge."

The Dramaturgical Perspective

In using the dramaturgical approach as an end point of analysis, this study of image manipulation will be centered in the communicative activities of a county chapter of the National Association for Mental Health, as it responds to the contingencies and constraints of its multiple interdependencies with other community organizations.

Our focal point is the activity of a team of actors known as the agency staff—a group of individuals who are cooperatively engaged in sustaining an impression that socially valued means are being used to achieve socially desired goals. With full responsibility for both verbal and nonverbal dramatization of the chapter's activities, this group of professionals not only manages its own performances, its members are also talent scouts, authors of scripts, prompters, stage managers, producers, and directors of the larger civic drama.

Specifically we shall attempt to describe why and to what extent the agency staff becomes a manipulator of information; how this activity is managed; and what its consequences are at the interpersonal, group, and societal levels. By conducting a case study of an agency which claims "to speak for those who cannot speak for themselves," we shall attempt to find out if the dramaturgical process increases the agency's effectiveness as a communication medium, or if the process, in fact, creates a communication barrier.

To attempt an analysis of all areas of agency activity is obviously beyond the scope of this study. Therefore, we shall begin with a description of the agency, its environment, and its organizational structure, and then move on to the dramaturgy of the day by day·routines as well as to the special effects used in the dramatization of programs involving a large number of volunteers and a high degree of community exposure.

And finally, we may even determine of what stuff heroes are made.

2
THE COMMUNITY CONTEXT

The city and county which shall both be called Pangloss comprise the nucleus of a sizeable metropolitan area. Despite the fact that the number of Panglossonians is rapidly approaching the million mark, the metropolis and its suburbs retain the insulated quality of those midwestern communities which are still surrounded by fertile farmlands.

Although the story is denied by the Chamber of Commerce, it is said that an airlines pilot, on his approach to the municipal airport, routinely announces: "Ladies and gentlemen, we will land at approximately 7:35 Central Standard Time. If your flight terminates here, you should set your watch back thirty years."

The pilot's observation may be apocryphal, but it is not without substance. Pangloss moved into the twentieth century reluctantly and has continued to lose momentum. During the first three decades, it barely survived a period of devastating political corruption; struggled, under the domination of a reform group, through the Great Depression and World War II, and reached the mid-century unprepared for the demands for dynamic adjustment. Like its State Legislature, the community habitually expends its energies debating trivialities, then stops the clock at 11:59 in an attempt to solve problems for which time has already run out. The collective self-deception has blocked much needed municipal improvement. There are no freeways, no convention centers, and few attractive hotels. The city has been known for the beauty of its homes, but its zoning board annually distinguishes itself by a near nationwide record in the granting of variances.

Although the prevailing nostalgia for the good old days is almost a functional derangement, the veneration for free enterprise and laissez faire economics has kept Pangloss attractive to business and industry. Thus, growth continues and Panglossonians are prosperous. Moreover, in comparison to other cities, it is extraordinarily homogeneous. There are relatively few Catholics, Jews, or ethnic representations; and the twenty percent of the population which is Negro is disproportionately middle class.

Frequently described as the last stronghold of the Protestant Ethic, the community and its old guard leadership have cherished a long tradition of opposition to urbanization, government interference, metropolitan planning, municipal recreation, freeway construction, aid to unwed mothers, federal school lunch programs, daylight savings time, and the undeserving poor. In addition to death and taxes, the citizens have the additional surety that there will arise an injunction-filing faction to halt or delay almost any proposed public work.

The above appraisal is a matter of record. Pangloss per capita income is one of the highest in the nation, but its expenditure on health, welfare, and recreation is one of the lowest. If, however, the community takes a dim view of "welfarism," it also holds a firm conviction that private philanthropy, with the support of the "independent sector" can "get the job done." There is a great deal of civic pride in the number of Pangloss-originated do-it-ourselves projects which have been cited in the *Reader's Digest*. There is also satisfaction in the continuing success of the United Fund campaigns.

Today in Pangloss, there are signs of new life. A young mayor—aggressive and politically astute—and his youthful administration are attempting to shift the tense of community thinking from past perfect to future progressive. However, this report deals with the first seven years of the sixties—a time in Pangloss when philanthropy remained a pleasant seasonal diversion, and the phrase "long hot summer" referred to good swimming weather.

The Subject

The Pangloss Mental Health Association is a United Fund agency and an affiliate of State and National Associations for Mental Health. The organization is not representative of the entire spectrum of community voluntary associations, but neither is it unique. More sophisticated than most, it has repeatedly won community recognition for the excellence of its public relations programs. However, the techniques by which it dramatizes its activities are commonly found among those organizations to whom the community has delegated responsibility for certain segments of public morality.

If the organization is not atypical, it may be a caricature of other such agencies. Its problems are representative, but they are also exaggerated. All social uplift organizations in the United Fund network share the exigencies of competing for the oftentimes capricious allocation of social resources. However, inasmuch as the Mental Health Association is relatively young (1949), it lacks the long tradition of service and respectability enjoyed by such groups as Family Service, Red Cross, or the Tuberculosis Association. It utilizes volunteer services to a greater degree than most agencies. And finally, although most benevolent organizations deal with problems which are to some extent stigmatizing, the stigma of mental illness is one which has been particularly persistent.

In spite of these and other problems, the agency has acquired a reputation for effectiveness. In the same year that *The Final Report of the Joint Commission on Mental Illness and Mental Health* questioned whether Mental Hygiene is a "diversionary movement or action group" (1961: 66-67), the Pangloss Mental Health Association won its first citation from the Metropolitan Services Council for "outstanding performance in effectively interpreting the agency program to the community."

The Association has also effectively conveyed to the United Fund its claim for increased support. In its first ten years of affiliation, its allocation was increased by more than 66%. Its annual budget is more than $100,000.

The Agency and Its Activities

For the mental health movement, 1961 was an historic year. The publication of the Joint Commission Report marked a watershed in the thinking of professionals. For more than a hundred years, largely as a result of the valiant efforts of Dorothea Lynde Dix, custody of mental patients had increasingly become a function of state institutions. But the mandate of the Commission was to return responsibility to the community. The notion of comprehensive mental health planning was born.

During the preceding decade, the Mental Health Association in Pangloss had formalized its activities. An office had been opened, a telephone installed, and the staff was growing larger. By the end of 1959, the agency had become sufficiently prosperous to expand its program and hire a press agent.

In the seven year period covered by this study, the professional staff of the Association consisted of a psychiatrically trained Executive Director, a Psychiatric Social Worker, and two Community Organization Directors who functioned in the overlapping areas of educational and volunteer programs, with public relations chores assumed by whichever role-encumbent was best qualified. The three clerical workers were shared by the "professionals," and from time to time, their efforts were augmented by office volunteers.

According to the bylaws, the governing body of the Association is a thirty-member Board of Directors—volunteers all—who are elected from a slate of candidates purportedly drawn from the membership by a nominating committee named by the President. Although the term of office is three years, ten of the thirty members are elected or reelected annually, thereby requiring a yearly reorganization.

Apart from the participation of these Board members, the Association staff depends to a large extent upon nonassociational volunteers for the implementation of programs. The "loosely bound mass of dues payers" to whom Selznick (1943) referred have become a casualty of United Fund restrictions on membership drives. Although the membership total ranges between two and three thousand, membership dues constitute a fraction of one percent of the budget. For the most part, individuals become members through a technicality which confers the status on anyone who designates for Mental Health the sum of one dollar or more of his United Fund contribution. Since a large portion of these designations are made by State Hospital employees at the request of their supervisors, the support is, at best, nominal. Moreover, although membership is a qualification for holding office, it frequently happens that a Board candidate is nominated and elected prior to his joining the organization.

Professed Goals and Agency Programs

According to the Articles of Association and Bylaws, the official goals of the Pangloss Mental Health Association are as follows:

(1) To work for the promotion and preservation of mental health and the prevention of mental illness.
(2) To raise the standards of care for those suffering from mental health disorders.
(3) To familiarize the public with the methods used in the care and treatment of persons who are emotionally or mentally disturbed.
(4) To disseminate accurate information to aid in carrying out the above objectives.
(5) To carry out in Pangloss County the accepted program outlined for county chapters by the State Association for Mental Health.

A pamphlet distributed by the Association describes its activities as falling into the five areas of (1) professional services, (2) legislative program, (3) research and training, (4) education, and (5) volunteer programs.[2]

Inasmuch as professional services are an encapsulated type of activity characterized by the one-to-one relationship of social worker and client, and since legislative activities and research and training programs are primarily directed and implemented by the State Association, we shall direct our attention to those programs oriented to the hospital and the community. The Association brochure describes them as follows:

Hospital Volunteer Activities

Direct service to patients in the state psychiatric hospitals and schools treating Pangloss County residents.

Operation Snowball—our gigantic annual project to collect thousands of gifts and bring Christmas to every hospitalized patient in psychiatric hospitals.

Educational Services

To help people develop a better understanding of the mentally ill, to help patients get earlier diagnosis and treatment, thus making recovery easier, it is necessary to reduce stigma and prejudice regarding mental illness. The Association provides speakers, films and literature for clubs, church and PTA groups on a wide variety of mental health subjects.

Workshops are planned for teachers, clergymen, police officials and other key groups.

A new area of agency activity which is arbitrarily and perhaps unfairly omitted is the program for student volunteers. However, this is a category of persons for whom I have considerable bias: their participation is authentic, energetic and enthusiastic; their values and relationships appear to constitute a different universe of social fact. Moreover, since their activities are segregated and are allotted only one half of one percent of the organizational budget, and since they are not permitted representation on the Association Board, it seems reasonable to confine the study to the portion of the membership which has a voice in the policies.

Previous Research

In the study of large scale organizations, much emphasis has been placed on the importance of organization structure in the preservation or displacement of professed goals. Structural functional analysis is a fruitful perspective for important contributions to organizational theory. However, it is possible that in neglecting phenomenological aspects, the structural functional viewpoint distorts—especially when it is applied indiscriminately to economic and noneconomic organizations.

A case in point is David Sills' study of the National Foundation for Infantile Paralysis. Ignoring the drama of polio, Sills (1957: Chaps. 1 and 2) attributes success to an organizational structure designed to maintain membership interest and an authority structure capable of resisting the internal processes of goal displacement.

If it is indeed structure which provides the success formula, it is significant that in selecting its new objective, the National Foundation considered—and rejected—mental health. According to the Foundation Executive Director Basil O'Connor,

> Tremendous pressure was brought to make this the extension of the program for the need is admittedly great. Yet of all the extensions of program considered, mental health proved to be the most difficult to develop [Joint Commission, 1961: 72].

If the problems of mental health could have been solved by structural reorganization patterned on the success formula of the National Foundation, it is doubtful that Mr. O'Connor and his associates would have passed over so challenging an opportunity. Admittedly the National Association for Mental Health has had crippling structural deficiencies. In a recent eight year period, it had no fewer than eight successive executive directors and acting directors. At its 1966 National Convention in New Orleans, new executive Brian O'Connell confided to a Staff Council committee: "We do not even know for sure how many chapters we have. We think it is between eight and nine

hundred, but we have not been able to get an accurate count"
(Field notes).

Historical Background

The dismal organizational failures of mental health
movements all the way back to Dorothea Lynde Dix have been
chronicled so well and so often that they do not bear repetition
(Joint Commission, 1961; also Beers, 1921, Deutsch, 1949,
Martin, 1959). The contemporary organization founded by
Clifford Beers has survived, but never has it become the
dynamic social movement its founder envisioned.

As the National Committee for Mental Hygiene, it was
organized in 1909 as a corporate structure—an arrangement in
which supervisory power resides in the national headquarters
and is delegated downward. Although by 1917 there had been
chartered seventeen state associations, the zest for organization
was never matched by a corresponding enthusiasm for funding.
As a result, the resources of these groups were too meager to
enable them to survive two wars and a depression, and by the
end of World War II, most of them had almost ceased to exist.

With the return to peacetime activities, the movement was
revitalized. In 1948, the state society was reorganized in
Pangloss, an office opened, and a staff provided; in 1949, the
first chapter of the State Association was organized in Pangloss
County. Both of these associations were going concerns prior to
the reorganization at the national level which created the
NAMH.

The existence of such "grandfather associations"—agencies
which predate the reorganization—has resulted in a powerful
group of autonomous state and county affiliates. Thus, the
Association's structure differs from state to state: in some cases

power is concentrated at the grass roots and leadership is delegated upward, in others, power resides in the state organization.

At the upper levels, the organizational chart approximates the typical pyramid with NAMH at the apex and eight regional directors serving in advisory capacities for the fifty states. At lower levels the chart becomes chaotic. There is no uniform pattern for the division of labor or delegation of authority, and lines of communication resemble the web of a drunken spider. Since NAMH provides no clearing house for program materials, communication is lateral with local chapters bypassing both state and national in the exchange of ideas and initiation of programs.

Philosophical Split

The fundamental problem of the national voluntary mental health movement has been its inability to reach a working consensus on either objectives or implementation of objectives. From its earliest abortive efforts, through Beers, and to the present, there has existed a philosophical split on the issue of whether the organization should be against mental illness or for mental health. That is, should it be a strong public pressure group dedicated to reform, or should it educate for "positive mental health?"

The bitterness of the controversy has not only prevented unified action, but has also created a situation in which advocates of each philosophy have career investments in projects designed to demonstrate the validity of their positions. Neither of the factions has advocated an either-or policy, but has principally been concerned with matters of emphasis.

Until very recently, the NAMH orientation was toward

education for mental health, with implementation directed to the production and distribution of pamphlets, plays, filmstrips, cartoons, TV programs, and comic books. As a means of preventing mental illness or effecting social change, the efforts have not been notably successful. In an early study of the organization, Kingsley Davis (1938: 55-65) noted:

> Mental Hygiene, being a social movement and a source of advice about personal conduct, has inevitably taken over the Protestant Ethic...not simply as a basis for conscious preachment, but also as the unconscious system of premises upon which its 'scientific' analysis and its conception of mental health itself are based.

Similar findings were made some twenty years later in a study by Gursslin, Hunt, and Roach (1959-60: 210-218). They concluded:

> The mental health movement is unwittingly propagating a middle class ethic under a guise of science .... If, as many sociologists and culturally oriented psychiatrists maintain, one of the primary roots of mental disorder lies in socially structured strains, then it may very well be that [it] is helping to support a system that is producing a high incidence of mental illness.

Although the Pangloss Mental Health Association participates in the distribution of NAMH literature, the thrust of its efforts has been directed to the involvement of volunteers in a wide variety of programs designed to create an awareness of needs and pressure for legislative change. The State Association, of which the PMHA is a chapter, has vigorously promoted the philosophy of voluntarism.

45

The point of this overview of history and development is simply that the National Mental Health Association has *never* had "an authority structure capable of resisting the internal processes of goal displacement, nor an organizational structure designed to maintain membership interest."

But it does not answer the fundamental questions. Are the developmental problems a consequence of the structure? Or is the structural weakness a consequence of developmental problems?

3
DEFINITIONAL DISCREPANCIES

The social improvement association, whether public or private, is by no means immune to goal-displacing activities arising from internal sources. For example, the pressure to be rational is both organizational and environmental in origin. However, in many cases, the pressure which produces the greatest amount of organizational drift is that which is generated by the discrepancies between the professed goals of the association and the dominant values of the environment.

The Mental Health Association, like many reform organizations, has as its principal concern those individuals who, by failing to conform to the norms which society considers desirable, have become stigmatized. The organization's ultimate objective is to establish the claim of this stigmatized category to humane treatment; but its proximate goal is to establish its own claim to environmental support so that it can survive long enough to accomplish its mission.

Now when there is an environmental demand for the good which an organization is attempting to produce, action which implements goals also implements survival. Thus, when there is no discrepancy between what clients appear to need and what contributors are willing to provide, an organization can project a pleasing image merely by making the public aware of its need-fulfilling proficiency. A case in point is Children's Bureau: by periodically publicizing pictures of proud adopters, this agency presents visible evidence of its effectiveness in making blessed an unblessed event. If the emphasis on the happy ending de-emphasizes (or obscures) the unsolved problems of infertility and illegitimacy, the Bureau is nevertheless achieving a goal for which it was established at a price which the public considers reasonable.

However, it is relatively rare that surplus and scarcity are counteracting dilemmas. The resolution of most social problems requires a redistribution of inequities in which the people who have may be less than eager to provide the resources for those who have not.

In the case of a social change organization, there is often a discrepancy between that which the organization considers desirable and that which is valued by the public. This value conflict may be relevant to means or to ends or to priorities. In any event, whether the philanthropic impulse is expressed in goods or services, it is contingent upon the donor's ability to perceive the need in terms consistent with his own values. Hence, to the extent that potential contributors define the values of an association as incompatible with their own, the mobilization of public support will depend upon the association's ability to reduce the definitional discrepancies.

To the people to whom this responsibility has been delegated there appear to be three possibilities for achieving a working consensus: the association may (1) change the values of the environment, (2) change the values of the organization, or (3) conceal the incompatibility of values by appearing to be what the public wants it to be.

Obviously, professed goals of the social change organization specify the first choice. In the following pages we shall show how societal pressure creates a strain toward the second, and how it comes about that the third alternative—image manipulation—appears to provide an expedient compromise. We shall be particularly interested in determining to what extent there is a relationship between the effectiveness of an organization and the amount of organizational energies directed to sustaining an acceptable image.

In linking effectiveness with authenticity, we are only peripherally concerned with how well the organization fulfills the set of requirements necessary for its survival. The critical questions are first, does the organization actualize its identity as an instrument of social change? And second, is it responsive to the human needs (Etzioni, 1968: 622-632) of its participants and of the community which it purports to serve?

STIGMA

In comparing the mental health movement to the polio crusade, the importance of stigma becomes evident. In the case of the National Foundation for Infantile Paralysis, there was little discrepancy between the goals of the association and the values of the environment. Unstratified, polio was a disease which killed and maimed "innocent victims" who attracted intense emotional identification. Although its high visibility and epidemic potential made it appear a formidable threat, its defeat could be effected with dimes, dances, and test tubes.

Few social agencies deal with problems possessing this fortuitous combination of characteristics. For the most part, instead of conducting popular crusades, they are concerned with troublesome situations where the "innocence" of the victim is not clearly established, the nature of "the enemy" is little understood, and total victory is not considered possible without a sacrifice disproportionate to the threat. The "battle" against mental illness is handicapped by all of these attitudinal encumbrances.

49

Unlike polio, which clearly belonged within the medical model, mental illness has traditionally been considered a character defect. Even when organic sources were first discovered, as in Bayles' identification of what is now known as paresis (1822),[1] the problem remained moral. The Korsakoff psychosis, identified in the late 1880's,[2] reinforced this attitude. Moreover, in the nineteenth and well into the twentieth century, the widespread notion that insanity resulted from masturbation was accepted even by the medical profession. An excerpt from the State Hosptial for the Insane Annual Report for 1851 says:

> Masturbation as a very fruitful cause for insanity deserves special attention. Fifty-five cases (out of 208) admitted during this last year we attributed to this cause, and we believe this to be less than the actual number. Many of these cases have been addicted to this horrid vice from youth, and even childhood, by which their mental and physical strength was insidiously debilitated and insanity slowly induced [Williams, 1950: 76].

Other "causes" listed in this same report include Reading Vile Books, Indulgence of Temper, Jealousy, Want of Occupation, Millerism,[3] Seduction, Intemperate Drinking, Mesmerism, and Excessive Use of Tobacco (Williams, 1950: 75).

Although psychoanalytic theory brought revolutionary changes in the thinking of mental health professionals and popularized the more interesting neuroses, the seriously disturbed disruptive individual continues to be rejected. According to a survey conducted by Elmo Roper in Louisville, Kentucky (1950), most people seek simpler interpretations. In Roper's sample, the majority (59.4 percent) believed that "the trouble with most people who are mentally ill is that they just don't want to face their problems" (Roper, 1950: 152-206). In Pangloss, ten years later, a Mental Health attitude study revealed that 85 percent of the people gave the "right answers" on questions measuring intellectual "understanding" of mental illness. However, on a question measuring social distance, 99 percent were emphatically unwilling to have a mental patient in their homes.[4]

Semantic Maneuvers

To combat the attitude that insanity is a characterological defect, the Mental Health Association has attempted to promulgate the idea that mental disorders are illnesses much like any other illness. This semantic maneuver has had a lip service success: the term mental illness has been accepted for polite social usage. Informally, however, the current usage of "sick," with a raised eyebrow inflection, clearly implies that this sick differs from normal sick.

Parsons' formulation (1957: 439-447) of the role of the sick and of the expectations defining the role provides some clarification. To play the sick role properly, the patient must admit that he is ill and must relinquish non-sick activities, must want to get well as quickly as possible, must seek competent help, and must cooperate with such help. To legitimate the definition of illness, he must behave in such a way that there can be no suspicion of malingering.

The majority of mental patients fail to meet one or more of these expectations and thus become double deviants. First, they fall short of meeting normal role expectations, and second, they compound their defections by their failure to be "properly" sick. The failure is not so much in the behavior of the patient as in the discernment of the public. Since most people do not recognize any but the most obvious psychotic behavior, symptoms which do not fit the stereotyped conceptions are often construed as wilfully inappropriate.

Lay reservations in regard to the "illness" concept are not without professional support. Dr. William Glasser, proponent of Reality Therapy, states (1965): "Because we do not accept the concept of mental illness, the patient cannot become involved with us as a mentally ill person who has no responsibility for his conduct." Psychiatrist T. S. Szasz (1960) terms the disorder "a myth whose function it is to disguise . . . the bitter pill of moral conflicts in human relations." In his sociological theory, Thomas Scheff (1966: 72-73) maintains that mental illness is a status rather than a disease. He describes it as an involuntary role performance which the individual plays "by articulating his behavior with the cues and actions of other persons."

To the general public, organic, psychogenic, and sociocultural theories of mental disorder have one outstanding characteristic: all are incomprehensible. If the source of public information is mass media, enthusiastic reports of "medical miracles" have probably contributed to the skepticism concerning the possibility of cure. Lobotomy, shock treatment, tranquilizers, psychic energizers and LSD—each has been hailed as a revolutionary breakthrough—but the need for funds and facilities does not diminish.

It is evident that in the case of mental illness, the victim is continuously discredited, whether by his own action, by societal attitudes, or, as Goffman has noted (1962: 148-169), by his therapist. The Joint Commission (1961: 58) sums up the resultant rejection pattern as follows:

> The reason the public does not react desirably is that the
> mentally ill lack appeal. They eventually become a nuisance to

other people and are generally treated as such . . . People do seem to feel sorry for them; but in the balance, they do not feel as sorry as they do relieved to have out of the way persons whose behavior disturbs and offends them.

But the mental patient's alleged unlovability is only half the problem:

The sight or thought of major mental illness, as our culture has come to understand it, stimulates fear—fear of what an irrational person might do [Joint Commission, 1961: 59-60].

The Mental Health Association's attempt to combat the stereotype of the madman, of the inherent violence of insanity, is largely nullified by mass media. J.C. Nunnally, Jr.'s study (1961: 74) of popular conceptions of mental health underscores the tendency of mass media to use imagery which reinforces the maniacal stereotype. Dimensions not included in the Nunnally analysis—dangerousness, unpredictability, and negative evaluation—are discussed by Scheff (1966: 70) in his description of bias in newspaper coverage. He notes that media give scant attention to statistics showing that ex-mental patients are less apt to commit crime than "normal" citizens, and further charges that selective reporting connecting former mental patients with violent and unpredictable acts "signifies the incurability of mental disorder."

The impact of this linking of mental disorders and violence, plus the vernacular references to all kinds of erratic behavior as crazy, mad, insane, etc., not only discredits the patient, but also suggests that since cure may not be sure, the only socially safe policy is continued custody—or, the status quo of containment. Further, as indicated by slang, the unreal world of the "funny farm" is perceived as populated by people who are so absurdly irrational as to be unaware of their own degradation.

In Pangloss, only 18 percent of 1,300 respondents (according to the Mental Health Survey) who had actually visited state mental hospitals rated them "poor." This, at a time when the average perdiem hospital expenditure was $4.76 per patient, and miserably crowded "treatment" facilities were visibly infested by roaches and rats.

THE COOLING PROCESS

In the battle against mental illness, as in many other battles, where victory appears to be remote and dear and containment is considered strategically possible, society tends to delegate this species of "dirty work" to the professional.

Thus, people who are actually or potentially socially disruptive become

> a kind of outgroup toward which we may have aggressive feelings and dislike ... although we profess to believe that they should not suffer restrictions or disadvantages. The greater their social distance from us, the more we leave in the hands of others a sort of mandate by default to deal with them on our behalf [Hughes, 1964: 32].

Although Everett Hughes' reference is to the delegation of punitive treatment, the let-George-do-it syndrome becomes frankly overt when the treatment is professedly humanitarian. The delegation of concern establishes the social agency as a kind of insulating medium which preserves or even increases the social distance between donor and deviant. And once this delegation has been made, society need no longer be embarrassingly involved with the individual tragedy of the unwed mother, the disadvantaged child, or the impoverished family.

In describing the delegation of concern as a "cooling process," we can find in Marshall McLuhan's (1965: 22-32) notion of "hot and cool media" a complementary conceptual scheme to Goffman's (1952: 462) definition of the "cooler." Goffman's cooler (the psychiatrist, the clergy, the social worker, the undertaker) functions to keep victims of the societal con game from "squawking"—to protect the system from the complaints of those who feel cheated until they can quietly accept their losses. McLuhan similarly defines the "cool medium" as "a censor which protects our central system of values . . . by simply cooling off the onset of experience a great deal."

The agency, then, which accepts the role of cooler, functions to protect societal values, and these values determine the organizational goals. It is an "informational cooling system" (McLuhan, 1965: 23) which substitutes detailed statistical reports for empathy-eliciting case histories. It preserves the status quo, it keeps the problem marginal, and there is no incompatibility of values.

In a complex society, the role of cooler is probably indispensable. Travelers' Aid provides a haven for the inevitable strays of a mobile population. Children's Bureau provides an orderly means for the transfer of infants from unwed to wed. And Scouting cools out the urban manchild by directing his explosive energies into the wide open spaces, or the den mother's basement. In these and other instances, professional competence and trained volunteers protect the interests of both those who give and those who receive.

But the state mental hospital system is ample evidence that the delegation of the humanitarian act is not always successful. In this event, the failure of the institutionalized cooling system provides the *raison d'etre* for a reform group.

Heating Up the Definition

Whether as a social movement or a formalized agency, the social change organization is, by definition, not a cooler but a warmer. Its goal is to convince society that the strategy of containment is detrimental, and thereby to stimulate action by influencing people to join in the action. To accomplish this objective, the organization will need to sustain a definition of the situation which enhances the desirability of the action and/or increases emotional identification with the object of the action.

Since empathic involvement with mental patients appears not to be achieved by calling their disorder "illness," an alternative means of enhancing the desirability of action is to amplify the magnitude of the threat. In this instance, the medium must be an information system providing the kind of data which creates cognitive dissonance. As defined by Leon Festinger (1957), dissonance is a psychological tension with motivational characteristics. It is aroused when one set of cognitions (i.e., "knowledges" or item of information) is contradicted by another set of cognitive elements.

In the case of treatment of the mentally ill, according to dissonance theory, if people are made aware of the incongruity between the humanity they profess and the inhumanity they tolerate, their discomfort should motivate them to change either their attitudes toward mental patients, or their attitudes toward treatment, or to modify both sets of attitudes. Hence, communications which increase the magnitude of the threat are designed to control the direction of the change. If an individual can be convinced that he or a member of his family may become a victim of the problem, there is a greater likelihood that his attitude change will be toward improved treatment. In other words, if the agency can communicate a heated up definition of the situation, it can more easily stimulate the desired action.

In a society whose theme is "cool it," the communication of such information is no small problem. In the health field, the situation seems to have created among the organized purveyors of problems an intense competition to be first worst. The Heart Association transforms its cold statistical mortality majority into the hot fact of "No. 1 Killer." Cancer Society, in a calculated bit of one upmanship, segments the statistics to lay claim to the title of "No. 1 Killer of Children." TB becomes the "No. 1 Killer among Contagious and Infectious Diseases." And since mental patients tend to die of old age, Mental Health remains in the dread disease contest by claiming that "one out of ten" will be victims of mental illness—the nation's "No. 1 Health Problem."

This heating up of statistics has become so commonplace that its effectiveness is greatly diminished. When the divisions and subdivisions of the morbidity and mortality tables are added to the threats posed by The Bomb, The Pill, Pollution, Unsafe Autos, God-is-Dead, LSD, etc., the capacity for anxiety becomes so overloaded that the system simply "turns off." Dissonance can be reduced by reducing the importance of all relevant elements together (Brehm and Cohen, 1962: 3-10).

Diversionary Action

Since competing information produced by the environment diminishes the effectiveness and contradicts the content of information produced by the Association, the utilization of purely verbal techniques as a means of changing societal values is to a large extent nullified. By the same token, the stigma which prevents people from vigorously supporting action for mental health also inhibits their participation in hospital volunteer programs designed to give them first hand information about problems and needs.

In such a case, where there is great competition for resources, and where the object of the action is considered unreliable, undeserving, or simply unapt, the organization must find other means of soliciting support and enlisting volunteers. The efficient solution for this problem is to define the action in terms compatible with the donor's individual values (prestige, status, economy, enjoyment) rather than his social values (concern for others). Thus, the agency minimizes the inconveniences of an inglorious battle and maximizes the opportunities for the enlistee. Instead of asking for commitment to the stigmatized victim, it seeks involvement with the agency itself.

While it is true that heating up the definition, as in the competition to be first worst, is a manipulative strategy, this manipulation of verbal symbols does not divert attention from either the action or from the object of action. By contrast, image manipulation—the glamorization of the organization—is specifically designed to seduce the volunteer—to give him the kind of impression that will lead him to act voluntarily in accordance with the agency's plan. It is a strategy which not only diverts attention, but also shifts the thrust of the action from the objects of action (the clients) to the actors themselves (the volunteers).

This deception is not initially a moral issue, but is rather perceived as an expedient means of achieving a favorable working consensus. It is a momentary bypassing of the ultimate goal of stimulating action in favor of the immediate imperative of mobilizing resources. Moreover, it is believed that by dramatizing the agency's performance, increased support will be attracted, the agency's influence will be extended, and ultimate goals will be more quickly attained. Since mobilization of resources is a legitimate and necessary activity in any instrumental organization, it is a process which should implement rather than replace goals. However, when mobilization becomes contingent upon enhancing the agency's image by satisfying the expectations of the volunteers rather than by responding to the need of the clients, the organization may become expressive rather than instrumental.

Whether or not this occurs will depend upon what constraints exist to keep the organization on target, and to what extent impression management can neutralize these constraints. Since we would expect constraints to exist within the organization as well as within the environment, it is necessary that we examine more closely the structural arrangements which determine the allocation of power and the delegation of responsibility.

4
THE FACADE OF
FORMAL ORGANIZATION

Civic drama is an omnibus term. It includes all of the various performances which are designed to sustain the impression that responsible citizens, using democratic processes, are voluntarily working together to achieve specific goals for the betterment of the community. The roles are played by unpaid volunteers, paid staff members, and miscellaneous others who become co-performers in an assortment of combinations.

Whether the performance is a production, carefully planned and rehearsed, or whether it is an ad libbed, improvised dramatization occurring when a performer is unexpectedly thrust "on stage," its success depends upon the extent to which these performance teammates are operating within a common frame of reference. Goffman (1959: 93) stresses the point that "if the team is to sustain the impression that it is fostering. . .there must be some assurance that no individual will be able to join both team and audience."

Ideally, this is true. However, the successful dramatization of the modern morality play necessitates a special audience-participation format. The star of the production is not a professional, he is "just a volunteer." He is Everyman. But as a role model, he is the best of Everyman. And he must be convinced—or act as if he were convinced—that the engineered performance is not a performance at all. Like a lay evangelist, he is expected to win converts to the cause.

While the real evangelist may count heavily on divine revelation and supernatural assistance, the philanthropic association tends to place its faith in the prescience and omniscience of staff. Since there are no sanctions provided for the control of an erring volunteer, the effective performance requires painstaking preparation of both performer and props. The staff-prepared script (unofficially, "the idiot sheet") consists of a detailed agenda, an inspirational message, appropriate anecdotes for the introduction of the speaker, and gracious acknowledgements of services rendered (with volunteers' names phonetically spelled).

A typical performance—one which may be witnessed during the philanthropy season (September through May) in almost any urban community on any day or evening, begins when the President of the Board rises from his seat at the speaker's table, adjusts the microphone, thanks the invocator, and officially opens the meeting with the predictable humor which is probably the only unscripted part of his performance.

Staff members listen apprehensively until the genuine (or polite) laughter subsides and the speaker says, "But seriously, ladies and gentlemen, I want to welcome you. . ." At this point, the Executive Director (seated with the guests rather than with the officiating volunteers) surreptitiously signals one of his Associate Directors (stationed near the control panel) and the volume of the public address system is increased, or decreased as indicated. The President continues in a glowing (staff written) tribute to the auspiciousness of the occasion (invariably noted as the first, the greatest, or the most outstanding event ever brought to the community). In conclusion, he says (with appropriate reverence):

> And now ladies and gentlemen, I want to introduce the man who is responsible for this great occasion. I am privileged to say that I have worked with this man on the Board of the Pangloss Mental Health Association for several years. I know

> from personal experience his dedication to this cause and the immeasurable leadership he has given our community in this great battle against mental illness. In spite of his busy schedule, he has attended many meetings, he has written many letters, and he has made many phone calls in planning and arranging this meeting. He has given countless hours—in fact, no one, no one but he knows how many hours he has given. Ladies and gentlemen, may I introduce our Conference Chairman. . . [Field notes].

As the chairman rises with measured dignity, staff members concentrate on joining the appreciative applause and carefully avoid each other's eyes. Mr. Chairman did attend three committee meetings, did make himself available for a ten minute consultation at his office between appointments, did permit his signature to be "forged" to staff-written letters, and did concur via telephone with staff plans and decisions.

When he graciously acknowledges his introduction, the knowledge that the ratio of staff hours to volunteer hours approximates seventy-five to one causes the staff project director a twinge of resentment. But she reminds herself that this is what she is getting paid for, while the real and unpurchasable contribution is the prestige of the volunteer's presence. And she admits further that his omission of any credit to staff is strictly according to script. He is a dependable and valuable teammate.

FORMAL ORGANIZATION

The above description is a standard opener for a wide variety of community action activities. Whether designed to raise funds, launch a project, appreciate volunteers, or educate citizens, the public performance features a prestigious volunteer in the role of protagonist with professional staff members unobtrusively occupying the status of backstage technicians. The arrangement is efficient. And it effectively fosters an impression of deeply involved community leadership.

In such a presentation, neither the disciplined selflessness of staff nor the apparent self aggrandizement of the volunteer necessarily stems from a deficient or abnormal need for recognition. Both have been socialized to accept the norms of the performance. These norms are not specified in the Board Manual. Instead they are the understandings which constitute the informal organization: the reciprocal arrangements through which role reversal permits a mutually advantageous working relationship.

If the outcome is an illusion, we can have no understanding of that illusion unless we examine the explicit reality on which it is constructed. Thus, for the purpose of analysis, our starting point must be the formal organization—"the system of rules and objectives defining the tasks, powers, and procedures of participants according to some officially approved pattern" (Broom and Selznick, 1963: 222).

According to the official bylaws, the Pangloss Mental Health Association membership governs itself through its chosen representatives—the Board of Directors. These thirty individuals are charged with the responsibility for all of the activities of the Association. This includes determining policy, conducting business, budgeting and fund disbursement, recruiting volunteers, program planning and evaluation, and employing, defining duties, setting salary, and supervising the Executive Director (Pangloss County Board Manual).

Implementation of Board responsibilities is a function of the Executive Committee and Standing Committees, in addition to special committees formed as necessary. The bylaws provide that all committee appointments shall be made by the President, and that each committee shall have Board representation (Pangloss County Board Manual).

Organization of Staff

The significance of this organizational arrangement stems from its *emphasis on the volunteer* as the locus of authority and the legitimated instrument for accomplishing the goals of the Association; and on its *de-emphasis of staff,* except as an adjunct for providing technical and professional assistance. The official communication channel which gives staff access to Board members only through the Executive Director clearly implies a distinct differentiation of status, and reinforces the official position that the role of staff is not to advise and propose, but to take direction. The exclusion of staff from Board meetings necessitates staff members' reliance on the Executive Director for both upward and downward interpretation of sentiment concerning any given activity.

This de-emphasis of staff is not consistent with either the qualifications or pay scales of the three staff associate directors. The position of Psychiatric Social Worker requires a Master's Degree and several years experience. And although the Volunteer and Education Directors are professional primarily by definition, all of the semi-professionals who have filled these positions have been career workers in community organization. Salaries are typical of those paid to professionals in the social agency field.

The Irrational Aspects of Rational Organization

The official, explicit set of rules that constitutes what is professed to be the formal organization provides a rational plan of implementation for an association characterized by a small group of enthusiastic volunteers with close interpersonal relationships and frequent interaction. However, as the Association increased in size and the programs increased in scope, the assumptions on which the structural prescriptions for volunteer roles were based became decreasingly valid.

The first assumption, that Board members can maintain communication with, and be responsive to the membership, is invalidated by the physical and social distances of an urban society. In its early years, the Association membership was composed of friends and relatives of mental patients—a highly motivated group of individuals united by a common bond of personal misfortune. After the initial period of growth, such a group reaches a plateau. If it is carrying on an agressive program, the small membership becomes overloaded with responsibilities. Books and records scattered throughout the city in the homes of members frustrate efficient organization. As the membership growth levels off, the limitations of the small group's power are recognized, hopes begin to fade, and factions develop.

Sooner or later, the membership realizes that to accomplish its objectives it must centralize its operation and enlist active support from outside the ranks of those who have been personally affected. This leads to the renting of an office and the hiring of someone to keep the books and answer the telephone.

Although this move to formalization is initially and manifestly designed to facilitate communication, its eventual and latent function becomes the preservation of social distance. As the organization grows, Board members are increasingly recruited from the upper influential levels of the community.

Since membership interest among the rank and file frequently develops as a result of direct or indirect experience with the health problem involved (Babchuk and Edwards, 1965: 152), it is not limited to the social strata ordinarily associated with philanthropic organizations. Thus, as social distance between members increases, the official communication channel of membership-to-Board comes to be abandoned.

In its stead, a sandwich type of communication structure develops in which the Board constitutes the upper crust, rank and file volunteers the lower, and between the two, spread thin, is staff—functioning as a medium of both integration and separation. It is important to note that although this arrangement is institutionalized, it is not given formal recognition. The organizational framework, as it is formulated in the official Board Manual, preserves the fiction that the Board is in direct communication with membership.

The second assumption, that Board members can and will assume responsibility for agency activities, is negated by the facts of volunteer participation. Numerous studies have shown that participation in voluntary associations is not an all-American activity, but is rather limited to a relatively small proportion of the population (Komarovsky, 1946: 686-698). In view of the fact that the willing are not always the desirable, the pool of resources becomes a relatively small puddle. And this scarcity of manpower is intensified by energetic interagency competition for the involvement of influential volunteers.

As only "part-time masochists," Board members have neither the time nor the inclination to handle the complexities of programs entailing months of preparation and the coordination of hundreds of volunteers. Further, the only formally specified role requirement which carries an official sanction is attending

Board meetings: failure to attend three consecutive meetings without an acceptable excuse can mean expulsion (Pangloss County Board Manual). Hence, the formal organization has no effective mechanism of social control to prevent default of responsibilities.

The assumption that the Association is Gemeinschaft in nature is clearly not consistent with the facts. The complexity is further complicated in that the PMHA is a part of not one, but two bureaucratic organizations. As a chapter of the State Association, it is constitutionally obligated to carry out in Pangloss County the accepted programs of the statewide organization, and to provide financial support (approximately forty percent of its allocation) to both State and National Associations. As an affiliate of the United Fund, it is subject to that organization's policies and practices. Since both of these organizations can wield controlling sanctions—revocation of charter on the one hand, disaffiliation or reduction of allocation on the other, the Association's autonomy is subject to severe limitations.

The retention of the Gemeinschaft formal structure in a Gesellschaft organization is not completely dysfunctional. In fact, it serves three important needs:

(1) It preserves the identity of the Association as a citizens' movement.
(2) It serves the agency's ideological position on the value of volunteer involvement.
(3) It provides a means by which the agency can increase its visibility and popularize its cause through prestige derived from the participation of community influentials.

However, to be a citizens' movement requires both citizens and movement, and the discrepancy between the demand structure (the role requirements) of the organization and the opportunity structure (the desirable resources) of the environment creates a situation in which having the one seems to preclude having the other. In short, the official structure provides no realistic means of implementing the official objectives.

Operationalizing the Formal Organization

To understand how this organization paradox is resolved we must part company momentarily with the conventional concepts of formal organization insofar as they relate to *official* procedures, rules, roles, and relationships.

If we reexamine the organizational arrangements, we see that the administrative problem stems from the fact that there are certain offices (Committee Representatives) which have been established and to which authority has been allocated and responsibility has been delegated. However, the filling of these offices by volunteers with varying degrees of interest and competency does not provide a means of implementing the work which needs to be done. On the other hand, the removal of incompetent incumbents would deprive the Association of the perceived benefits of the officeholder's ability to confer his prestige on the organization.

The administrative response to this problem is to retain the volunteer incumbent, but to compensate for his inadequacies by assigning his defaulted responsibilities to a paid employee—a solution which has the effect of *giving every office double occupants*. Thus, every Board Committee Representative has a staff implementor, and every staff member is assigned responsibility for the effective performance of from three to seven Board Committees. However, although this arrangement is accomplished by explicit job descriptions formulated by the Executive Director and the Personnel Committee, *the delegation of responsibility is not given official recognition* as a part of the formal organization. Instead it remains a private arrangement to sustain the public image of the citizens' movement.

If, therefore, we take officially sanctioned arrangements as our organizational criteria, we see that what is professed to be the formal organization is actually a front. And the real formal organization is the rationally planned delegation of responsibility which is designed to accomplish the organizational goals while maintaining the front.

With apologies for mixed metaphors, the formal organization may best be compared to an iceberg: the prestigious volunteers comprise the upper section, a visible and sparkling evidence of free-floating philanthropy; but hidden beneath the surface and supporting the weight are the mercenaries and foot soldiers of the citizens' crusade.

Thus we have a single structure of action. Since the Board receives recognition and staff receives pay, the double occupancy of offices is a planned, sanctioned arrangement. Superficially, this arrangement appears not to differ significantly from any bureaucratic organization in which there is a policy making body (the Board), management (the executive and standing committees), staff (the paid technicians), and workers (the rank and file volunteers). However, according to Weber, in the conventional bureaucracy, authority is distributed in a stable way.[1] Merton (1957: 195) says:

> In such an organization there is integrated a series of offices,
> of hierarchized statuses, in which inhere a number of

obligations and privileges closely defined by limited and specific rules. Each of these offices contains an area of imputed competence and responsibility. Authority, the power of control which derives from an acknowledged status, inheres in the office.

In other words, in the rational organization, each person is (ideally) given a range of authority which is related to his range of responsibility. By contrast, in the PMHA, responsibility is delegated to staff, but there is no *acknowledged status* commensurate with the responsibility. Therefore, behind the facade of the formal organization is an institutionalized system which not only changes its communication structure, but also results in an *almost total bifurcation of authority and responsibility.*

This does not mean that all authority remains with the Board and all responsibility goes to staff. But it does mean that the responsibility which is defaulted to staff is without legitimate authority. And it is this fact which provides the basis for the informal organization.

The Informal Organization

Although the retention of authority by the Board and the delegation of responsibility to staff creates awkward organizational complexities, it is an arrangement which can be operationalized. In its superordinate position, the Board, theoretically at least, can recruit, train, delegate, and direct staff members. And by exercising its powers of sanction, it can control.

However, there is a complicating factor. According to the Board Manual, the role of staff is "to help implement the policies and programs as outlined by the Board and Committees and in doing so, maintain continuity from one year to the next." The assumption that the function of maintaining continuity will be a byproduct of implementation is somewhat naive.

In the conventional business or industrial association, where authority is legitimated by knowledge and expertise, the maintenance of continuity is a function of management. Thus, staff may come and go, but the administration assures stability through established mechanisms of recruitment, socialization, and sanctions.

In the Pangloss Mental Health Association, the situation is quite different. Here, authority is legitimated by incumbency in office and it is the employee who has the knowledge and expertise. Further, since the Board of Directors is reorganized annually, it is management which comes and goes and the employees who must train (and sometimes even select) the administration.

When volunteer leadership either cannot or will not exercise authority or accept responsibility in these areas, and when it does not maintain communication with the rank and file, staff members' assumption of the defaulted responsibilities and their exercise of unlegitimated authority creates an informal organization which is a mirror image of the formal organization facade.

In the following description of the performances and the performance mechanisms, we will show how the dramaturgical process makes possible a reversal of the superordinate-subordinate positions of volunteers and staff.

5
THE CASTING OF CIVIC DRAMA

The selection, socialization, and control of a superordinate is at best a delicate procedure. Among social agencies, the official name for this process is "developing community leadership"; but the unofficial, or backstage term is "nursemaiding the volunteer." According to Goffman (1959: 102) it is accomplished as follows:

> Whenever inexperienced or temporary incumbents are given formal authority over experienced subordinates, we often find that the formally empowered person is bribed with a part that has dramatic dominance while the subordinates tend to direct the show.

But there is more involved here than bribery. By relinquishing dramatic dominance to the volunteer, staff is provided a front to cover its use of unauthorized power. At the same time, by defaulting directive dominance to staff, the volunteer can maximize his contribution and minimize his investment. Hence, the efficiency of the activity provides the rationalization for the deception. In addition, since staff is paid in cash while volunteers receive only personal satisfaction, the volunteer is encouraged to overrate his "real" contribution. This is known as "making the volunteer experience meaningful." By "providing a sense of participation" staff can effectively foster the impression that no impression is being fostered.

Although the arrangement appears to give the volunteer a great deal of status at the expense of staff, the status gained is not without risk. Any public meeting is a gamble. The speaker may be dull. The audience may be hostile. And the appreciation ritual invariably results in unfortunate omissions. Even in so limited a performance as a planning session, the staff member's plans, presented in the volunteer's own words, may create a polarizing controversy. But by relinquishing stardom, staff can, to some extent, remain neutral and avoid blame.

Goffman (1959) cites a comparable example in his description of the British Infantry in World War I:

> . . . experienced working class sergeants managed the delicate task of covertly teaching their new lieutenants to take a dramatically expressive role at the head of the platoon and die quickly in a prominent dramatic position.... The sergeants themselves took their modest place at the rear of the platoon and tended to live to train still other lieutenants.

In effect, the performance is built around amateurs who may have little or no orientation to the agency philosophy or to the role in which they have been cast. That professional staff remain in the background is an inflexible rule designed to foster the impression that all action is carried forward by the enthusiastic efforts of unpaid amateurs as a part of a militant social movement. It does not mean that the volunteer is incapable of making a real contribution, nor does it necessarily imply that he is duped by the staff. It is simply that, under pressure to be rational, there is greater efficiency in using the volunteer as a front than there is in utilizing his talents for planning and directing the activities in which he takes part.

VOLUNTEER TYPOLOGIES

Since casting is vital to the successful performance, it is essential that staff members have sufficient information about their potential teammates to predict what quality and quantity of performance may be expected. Sills' typology of volunteers—Good Citizens, Joiners, Polio Veterans, and Humanitarians—is ambiguous when applied to Mental Health. Not only is it ineffective for prediction, but it also violates the Mental Health staff rule: "Never question the motivation of a volunteer!" This rule is overtly observed; however one staff member said:

> Of course you speculate—at least in your own mind—about their motivations. But it really isn't very important. The fact is, they're here and we need them. I don't care how miserable their motivation is. If I can make it accomplish something good—at least, what I think is good—thenwhat difference does it make [Field notes].

What does appear to make a difference, in performance as well as commitment, is the volunteer's reference group. The question—with whom does he identify?—used as a clue for classification, provides the key variable as well as a means of describing without overt value judgment. In the Mental Health Association, staff experience suggests the following typology of five categories for adult volunteers.

The Pariahs

The first two categories include those persons whose intimate experience with mental illness has given them an outcast status in a society of "normals." The professional pariah is the ex-mental patient who becomes a "hero of adjustment" (Goffman, 1963: 25) by publicly acknowledging his stigmatized status. The peripheral pariah is the individual, who, by being related to a mental patient, shares his discredit—"the courtesy stigma" (Goffman, 1963: 10). Both types identify with the patient, and because the agency is perceived as sharing their concern for improving treatment and reducing stigma, they may be counted upon to commit themselves to the Association's ultimate goals.

The professional pariah is viewed by staff with both hope and apprehension. As a live warm demonstration of the slogan "The Mentally Ill Can Come Back!" this person, if articulate and attractive, is both valuable and rare. But he is also considered potentially disruptive and especially vulnerable to pressure situations. If he is given wide publicity and exposure there is a boomerang effect if he relapses. There is also the question of the existence of a positive relationship between his willingness to exploit his ex-patient role and his propensity for recurrent mental illness.

The peripheral pariah is considered to be more dependable and more apt to view the Association as a panacea—expecially if he has a close relationship to a patient. Where the professional pariah hinges his entire identity to his role, the relative or friend of the patient tends to view his commitment in moral terms—as a kind of "calling"—often in the religious sense. A typical statement is: "I finally decided that the reason I was chosen to bear this burden was so that I might better understand and help others."

Aware that this volunteer will have guilt feelings if he refuses an assignment, staff tends to draw him into deeper and deeper involvement. He becomes an insider, a part of the "we" group. One such volunteer, who has been active in the Association for more than ten years, expressed it ruefully and graphically: "First they lick you all over and then they swallow you whole."

A somewhat different type of peripheral pariah is the professional mental health worker who is employed elsewhere in the community. Included here would be the psychiatrist, psychologist, social worker, clinician, and psychiatrically oriented clergyman. Because his share of courtesy stigma has been voluntarily accepted, it is minimal. He is also more detached and his view of the Association is objective and critical. He, too, feels a moral commitment, but it is professional rather than personal. He is very capable of resisting overinvolvement, but even his token performance is valued for the prestige and legitimation which his profession lends the agency.

The Career Volunteers

This third set consists of people for whom participation is either a career in itself or an avocation related to business or professional interests. Consisting of socialites, business executives, or professional people, the category contains individuals whose reference group is the establishment, and whose commitment to the agency will be contingent upon the upward or downward direction of their status as "movers and shakers" in the community. They are dependable, professional and detached; their relationship to staff ranges from coldly exploitative to warmly impersonal. They are quite cognizant of "the need for good public relations," and if they are men, are apt to express the opinion that "this organization should be run like a legitimate business!" Proficient in volunteersmanship, they know the rules of the game and play it with sophisticated ease. They consider themselves, and are considered by staff, to be leadership caliber. Since theirs is a rational approach, they expect staff support and rarely demand the opportunity to "do it my own way." They may be counted upon for a professional performance with a minimum amount of rehearsal.

Good Works Volunteers

The fourth classification is composed of persons who are members of religious and philanthropic organizations, some- times expressive groups who are trying to justify their existence by community service. As volunteers they maintain their group identification and tend to be committed to the Association only so long as a competing worthy cause does not capture their sympathy. They are primarily interested in working directly with patients, or in raising funds for projects which will directly benefit patients. If they do hospital work, their allegiance is generally transferred to the hospital. As long as they have no problems they expect little staff support or interference. They view the agency as a provider of projects—a middleman whom they would prefer to circumvent.

For the most part, good works volunteers are dependable individuals whose self-sufficiency and disinterest in personal status preclude their involvement as members of the per- formance teams. Moreover, since they frequently insist on working as a group of twenty or more under the banner of their own organization (e.g., the Evangelical Add-A-Couple Class), their effectiveness is limited to those projects in which batch involvement is feasible. The "witnessing of Christianity to the community" effects little church-influenced change when the effort is predicated on enhancing the denominational image.

Occasionally, secular organizations view working with mental patients as a source of thrills and excitement. One such group was an association of female civil defense workers. Apparently attempting to find some way of filling the long, long hours (while waiting for mass disaster), they rejected all proffered projects as "just not exciting enough to keep the ladies interested."

The Loners

The final classification consists of individuals who identify with neither the organization nor the establishment. Intelligent, energetic, capable, and highly task oriented, they have a considerable immunity to manipulative strategies. The typical loner has limited patience with bureaucratic rigidities, is quick to discern the chinks in a facade, and does not sidestep confrontation. His penchant for publicly posing the embarrassing question makes his inclusion on the performance team a high risk asset. If he represents a powerful interest group, or has attracted a sizeable following, he may be co-opted for board membership. However, if he is without influence, he is labeled "troublemaker" and quietly dropped.

A subtype in the loner category is the prima donna. Often this is a woman who appears to have no relevant affiliation. Like an orphan virus looking for a disease, she enthusiastically attaches herself to a cause. Given a committee chairmanship, she sets unrealizable goals, and failing, sets about to restructure the organization which she feels has failed her. Although her criticism also is relevant to organizational inflexibility, she subjectively directs her attack toward the inadequacies of paid personnel. Staff considers her ego needs to be insatiable; her relationship to employees is that of mistress to handmaiden; and her expectations of staff support are impossible to fulfill.

Because she identifies with authority, she takes her complaints directly to the top and becomes disillusioned with the entire organization if severe penalties are not exacted for all alleged offenses. Briefly a friend, she is forever an enemy—but by the time staff learns that her history of disruptive activities includes many other agencies, it is usually too late to avoid conflict.

Both the staff of Mental Health and staff members of other agencies agree that the Association attracts a disproportionate share of such volunteers. It is speculated that these people give service to get service—that they join Mental Health in the hope that some of it will rub off.

If all lone individuals who join the Association could be placed in the "troublemaker" category, many problems could be anticipated. However, the loner classification is a catchall. Frequently, persons who are misclassified here actually belong among the pariahs and become deeply committed volunteers. Others quietly serve the Association for years, asking nothing in return.

One such volunteer, known as "the cookie lady" has provided nearly one thousand dozen cookies for the Association's use at hospital ward parties. Although she has never publicly identified with the agency, she has, without fail, baked seven dozen cookies every month—except December, when she bakes seventeen dozen. The activity has been sustained over a ten year period.

Overlapping Categories

Staff members tend to assume that anyone who gives such long term active service is in reality a covert pariah. However, there are some instances of overlapping categories where the stigmatized status is acknowledged but is a secondary aspect of volunteering. One young man, typed as a career volunteer, frankly admitted:

> My company not only expects, but insists that every junior executive be involved in community service—and Personnel puts it all on the record. Since my brother has been in and out of psychiatric wards for the past ten years, I chose Mental Health. But hell, I even get brownie points for teaching Sunday School. [Field notes].

The omission of the classification "Humanitarian" is less an expression of cynicism than of cautious optimism. One staff member said, "You always hope for the best—but if you expect the worst you don't get hurt." For staff members to preserve the belief that everyone is basically a humanitarian is not especially difficult. They remind themselves that in Pangloss there are many ways of gaining status which are more rewarding than volunteer work in the private agency field. However, the consensus is that the best volunteers are those who have least status anxicty:

> The ones who aren't trying to prove something are the ones who are willing to roll up their sleeves and pitch in on anything that needs doing. The climber doesn't dare. It's funny, but doctors often seem to be the most insecure—stuffier too. The psychiatrist who cuts out of a Saturday meeting tells you he has "an appointment at the University"—but he doesn't say it's on the 40 yard line [Field notes].

STAFF TYPOLOGY

For the most part, volunteers classify staff members in two categories: those who are dedicated, and those who "sit around drinking coffee." Staff members themselves, since they are not responsible for the selection of their colleagues, and since every staff colleague is, for better or worse, a part of the team, tend to regard their fellow workers as either dependable or undependable teammates. However, for performance purposes, these persons fall into classifications much like those of the volunteers.

Pariahs and loners exist in both groups. On staff, the counterpart of the career volunteer—i.e., the worker who identifies with the establishment—is the community organization specialist. And the psychiatric social worker, who is oriented to the client rather than to the organization, is regarded much like the good-work volunteer.

The principal difference, of course, between staff and volunteers, is in the degree of professionalism. With volunteers, willingness and influence are the prime determinants of recruitment; while with staff, the determining criterion is competence. When the sanction is salary rather than appreciation, the agency is better able to recruit selectively, to socialize effectively, and to transform the recruit into a dependable performer.

But the recruitment mechanism sometimes fails to provide a plastic individual who can be molded to the institutional model. The probability of failure is perhaps greatest among the ex-mental patients who become professional pariahs, and among the loners whose personality characteristics appear to prevent their successful assimilation into any organization.

At one time during the study, there were three employees on the State and Pangloss staffs who were ex-patients. The two individuals who most vigorously exploited their pariah status experienced serious psychotic episodes and subsequent re-hospitalization. The third former patient terminated employment on the advice of her psychiatrist. In one of the cases, the employee became disturbed during a highly publicized agency campaign, combined forces with a disturbed (and later re-hospitalized) ex-patient member of the Board, and managed to create a disruption which ultimately involved a state official's wife, a United Fund Allocations Committee member, and the entire PMHA Board. The diagnosis of mental illness was not made for either the employee or the Board member until after an executive's job was threatened and county and state organizations were severely shaken. (Since that time, the Association has modified its policy of special consideration for the employment of ex-patients, and equal opportunity is now extended to normals.")

There has also been a high incidence of emotional disturbance or history of disturbance among clerical employees. Within the time period of the study, among persons who had worked for PMHA, there was one suicide and one known suicide attempt. At any given time during the study, there was at least one secretary on staff who was "in therapy" or who had a psychiatric history.

There are several possible interpretations. First, the agency's professed position—that the mentally ill can be rehabilitated—obligates it to a bias toward hiring those who arc attempting a comeback. Second, people who are involved in a health association may be more apt to seek professional help sooner and more frequently than individuals who are less aware of symptoms and treatment facilities. Third, it is possible that agency pressures are, of themselves, alienating. And finally there is the possibility of self selection.

Unquestionably, self selection is applicable to the pariahs. However, regardless of the motivation of the employee, the presence of people who have had, are having, or need therapy is complicated by the psychiatric orientation of the agency. The permissive attitude tends to regard any display of temperament as a temporary emotional disturbance, and employees may safely ventilate their feelings. Furthermore, even when a temporary disturbance is prolonged, there is great reluctance to attach the label of mental illness to an employee. In part, this is due to genuine concern. But it is also related to the effects on the agency image: for the Mental Health Association to give the impression that it generates mental illness does not inspire confidence.

The situation contributes little to discipline or harmony among clerical employees, and professional staff spends a disproportionate amount of time mediating secretarial conflicts. But to attribute the problems of tension management to the personal insecurities of the involved individuals (whether professional or clerical) is to suggest that Mental Health has an uncommon allure for the socially inept. However interesting this notion may be, it is a superficial explanation.

Initially, we suggested that in sustaining the imagery of the civic drama, the division of labor created an uncertain alliance in which both amateurs and professionals play discrepant roles. Therefore let us look at these roles and attempt to identify the sources of role strain.

RECRUITMENT OF STAFF

In the recruitment process, the opportunity structure of the agency is both prescriptive and proscriptive for available resources. Inasmuch as the salary scale of social agencies is below that of business, industry, and most professions, the system primarily attracts action-oriented idealists. Some of these individuals have been motivated by experience with the stigma of mental illness, but most employees are recruited from other community agencies. Ordinarily, neither type has had extensive experience in social change organizations; and both tend to have great faith in the power of education. If they are ambitious, Mental Health appears to be a field in which a minimum of effort can accomplish much, and great effort should bring about revolutionary change. They tend to perceive the agency as promising the simultaneous realization of humanitarian ideals and a gratifying career.

The True Believer

Since the self which appears to await the recruit in this staff role is in many ways consistent with his ideal self, he is readily converted to a True Believer (Hoffer, 1951). Exposure to the needs of patients, confrontation with the hopelessness of the back wards, and observation of the real or apparent apathy of the hospital staff, are highly motivating experiences. In learning, the recruit is moved; consequently, he perceives the Mental Health philosophy of involvement as a supremely logical means of moving others. In his initial enthusiasm, it is not difficult for him to become convinced that the agency is the only hope and the only instrument of power for accomplishing the needed change.

85

In the formalized social movement, the fanatical participation which characterizes the zealot is tempered by the rational processes through which the individual chooses a career. However, in Mental Health, the recruitment process and initial socialization are designed to produce a dedicated worker and high staff morale. According to Blumer (1951: 167-222), such morale is based on a set of convictions which have the character of a religious faith. The convictions are of three kinds: (1) conviction of the absolute rectitude of the purpose of the movement, (2) faith in the ultimate attainment of the goal, and (3) belief that the movement is charged with a sacred mission. The Mental Health indoctrination process produces these convictions, and the recruit sincerely believes in his new role.

SINCERE RECRUIT TO DEDICATED CYNIC

To remain sincere, an employee must be protected from the realities of civic drama. But since he cannot retain his naivete and become an effective member of the performance team, his continuing socialization requires that he be initiated into backstage rites and be acquainted with dramaturgical secrets. He must exchange idealism for pragmatism, but he must also keep the zeal of the True Believer. These expectations are not incompatible. According to Goffman (1959: 18):

> When an individual has no belief in his own act we may call him "cynical" reserving the term "sincere" for individuals who believe in the impression fostered by their own performance . . . .
>
> It is not assumed, of course, that all cynical performers are interested in deluding their audiences for the purposes of what

is called "self interest" or private gain. A cynical individual may delude his audience for what he considers to be *their own good,* or *for the good of the community, etc.*

In making the transition from sincere recruit to dedicated cynic, the employee does not lose his conviction of the rectitude of the movement, but he does begin to see himself as a member of an in-group which is endowed with special insight and moral superiority. Unlike the fanatic, he is not contemptuous of the unconverted. Instead, he has faith that he can use their "miserable motivation" to accomplish their conversion.

While the loss of innocence is inevitable, it is not without compensation. Acceptance into the inner circle provides identity and in-group status. Effectiveness in fostering impressions wins the admiration of co-workers. And mastery of the art of getting people to enjoy doing what one wants them to do provides an exhilarating sense of power.

The manipulatory dramaturgical devices are made respectable by the public relations idiom. The "agency image" is treated as a transcendental value and ultimate referent. A program is evaluated "policywise" in terms of its "P.R. potential" or "publicity mileage." Programs are "sold" or "promoted"; and "contacts" are "cultivated"—especially if they are "live ones."

Thus, the stationery letterhead, a volunteer's voluptuousness, the secretary's credit rating, and the executive's galoshes, all come to be evaluated in terms of their relevance to the image. To enhance the image is to build a better mousetrap. But it is more efficient. It requires nothing concrete.

If the employee is repulsed by the deceptive and manipulative aspects of his role, there is a ready rationalization: "Of course we *use* people—we have nothing else to use." This

87

manipulation of people "for their own good" or for the good of the community is not unlike the definition of the situation which regulates the behavior of employees in a mental hospital (Goffman, 1962: 93). By defining anything that staff does as therapeutic, and any resistance as symptomatic of pathology, the agency actors can keep the faith in the social desirability of their action. Moreoever, when manipulation is the norm, the nonmanipulator is the deviant.

Not every employee is able to remain a True Believer and dedicated cynic. For some, the initial commitment and the euphoria accompanying successful manipulation do not diminish; but for others, there is ambivalence and progressive disenchantment. This is not so much loss of faith in the sacred nature of the mission, as disaffection with the means of grace.

6
GHOST ROLES AND ANCHORED IMAGERY

When a staff member is given the responsibility for an agency program which is a straightforward representation of an acceptable reality, the role can be performed with minimal strain and relationships with volunteers can be open and honest.

As an example, the Association's Hospital Volunteer Program is very nearly what it professes to be, and there is little discrepant information to be concealed.

In this program, activity is oriented to the ultimate goals of the Association. By working in mental hospitals, volunteers have an opportunity to gain insight into the nature of mental illness, are exposed to the needs of patients and hospitals, and provide direct and supplementary stopgap services which, if they do not meet needs, at least provide a diversion for the patient. In addition, in most cases the hospital volunteer chairman is one who accepts responsibility for her office. In short, it is truly a volunteer program, there is genuine enthusiasm, and legitimate means achieve legitimate goals.

However, most people perceive this type of volunteering as an educational device which threatens to tell them more than they really want to know. The hospital volunteer may be a heroine to her bridge club, but for her friends, the stereotyped conceptions of mental illness tend to reinforce a preference for "safer" types of altruistic action.

Thus, to provide a volunteer with the meaningful experience he seeks, to avoid the "asking too much" which may repel rather than attract, the Association, like many other agencies, gears its activities to the norm of most-least. In other words, by promising the most satisfaction for the least effort, it can maintain a favorable position in interagency competition.

A second problem with the Hospital Volunteer Program is that because it is difficult to accomplish en masse, it has low visibility and limited publicity potential. Since the agency's dependence upon philanthropy requires it to provide the United Fund Allocations Committee *measurable* evidence that its stewardship of the donor dollar is exemplary, there is risk in any approach which does not lend itself to impressive quantification.

To minimize this risk, and at the same time to involve volunteers in activities which keep them comfortably distant from patients, the community education project is ideal. It provides opportunities whereby substantial numbers of volunteers can serve on planning committees, and community leaders can be publicly exhibited before community audiences.

The Professional Mystique

That workshops, seminars, educational conferences, and annual meetings are well within the scope of volunteer talent is demonstrated daily by such associations as League of Women Voters, PTA, church groups, etc. However, when an association has been formalized and concern delegated, a professional mystique develops in the socialization of staff. The volunteer becomes a part of the out-group. It is assumed that he will not be able to understand the intricacies of agency philosophy or United Fund policy.

This attitude of staff was inadvertently, but appropriately, expressed by a speaker at a United Fund Public Relations

Conference. In a glowing tribute in which he mixed metaphors with abandon, he said: "It may be staff that puts this thing on wheels, but you've got to remember: it's the volunteers who *grease the tracks*" (Field notes).

The possibility of creating an image of a social movement with spinning wheels is avoided in the PMHA by the executive edict: "Don't ever assume that anybody knows anything!" Thus, volunteers are guided, directed, and stimulated in the making of the plans which staff considers desirable. Every dramaturgical device for assuring an undisrupted performance is employed and nothing is taken for granted.

Directive Dominance

Since the directive dominance of staff lies in its ability to control information, a staff member can become superordinate only to the extent that he can exercise such control. In the Pangloss Mental Health Association, official access to information is determined by rank; however, in some agencies, staff, director, and board members work as partners with near equal status and open recognition of the special contribution made by each. A former PMHA employee, now on the staff of such an agency, said:

> You just can't imagine the difference. Here I am a person in my own right—and my contribution is recognized as the contribution of a professional in the field. I play a real honest-to-God role—not a ghost role. It's delightful to work with, rather than for, volunteers [Field notes].

As indicated in the above remarks and in the previous discussion of the formal organization, status ascribed to staff roles in the Mental Health Association is determined by a rigid hierarchy of rank. The fact that only the Executive Director ordinarily attends Board meetings places him as the only employee with near equal status to the Board. In addition, his control of information to and from the Board enables him to keep his Associate Directors in positions of dependency in their roles as staff performers.

While this great degree of status differentiation gives the Executive the directive authority over nearly every facet of a performance, it also places upon him the full responsibility for the success of that performance. And if his position is reinforced by his ability to withhold information, it is also made more vulnerable. A staff member who is ignorant of the "official line" for a given occasion, who must ask for consultation before taking a public stand, is also a staff member who may inadvertently disclose destructive information. Thus, in his solo role, the Executive must be confident of every detail. An Associate Director commented:

> When a Board member starts telling you how he feels about a policy you haven't even heard of, all you can do is fake it. I'm sure that sometimes we didn't communicate simply because we were so busy. But mostly, we were treated as if we did not have the discretion to handle Board level information [Field notes].

The situation creates resentment and distrust. Although there was never any evidence—either real or hearsay—that the Director unfairly claimed credit or diverted blame, Associate Directors persistently believed that helpful information was withheld for devious reasons. Some of this feeling stemmed from the Executive's secretiveness. For example, Board minutes were treated as highly classified information. Yet staff members invariably managed to get copies and invariably found them uninformative. That pains were taken to conceal trivia only reinforced the suspicion of devious intent.

Since the withholding of information increased social distance between staff and Board, it also created status anxiety. Socially, staff members' rank equalled that of the majority of volunteers; but professionally, their rank was depressed. One staff member expressed the feeling as follows:

> It kills you. You get to feeling that you are absolutely a nothing—simply dirt. But I have a defense. When they start treating me like a servant, I find some nice casual way to remind them that I live farther north than they do. Or I happen to mention a social event that I went to that they didn't [Field notes].

By failing to share essential information, and by retaining the prerogatives of directive dominance, the executive may safely delegate responsibility only when a reality may be safely exposed. Since the citizens' movement must appear to be self-propelled rather than pushed by staff, the ghost role requires ingratiation and self-effacing behavior. And since directive dominance is retained by the executive, associates have little autonomy. The ideal self which appeared to be waiting in the role is elusive.

ANCHORING THE IMAGE

Whether a volunteer is seduced into relinquishing directive dominance to paid personnel, or whether he is knowingly participating in the civic drama, he requires assurance that the action he is taking will not be personally disadvantageous. Thus, the agency staff must produce its own performance for the purpose of enticing members of its volunteer audience into on-stage participation.

The recruitment act consists of many routines and is staged in many settings, but by and large the imagery of the organization is anchored to the permanent set known as The Association Office. It is here that staff members can star in their own scenes, here that the staff front is fabricated.

Goffman (1959: 27) defines the front as the expressive equipment of a standard kind intentionally or unwittingly employed by the individual during his performance. The setting consists of the scenic parts of expressive equipment, while the personal front is described as the appearance and manner of the performer.

In Pangloss, nearly all United Fund agencies are situated in an office complex known as The Good Samaritan Foundation Center. Before the wrecker's ball demolished the deteriorating dwellings of its neighbors, the grey stone facade of this private philanthropy headquarters was overshadowed on three sides by soot-grimed tenements. Today, the building stands aloof and alone, the only survivor of a massive slum clearance project. A local clergyman describes it as "formidable." He said:

> I never go there but what I wonder about the poor people it is supposed to serve. You walk into that cold empty lobby, search for the agency you need on the wall directory, then hope that the self service elevator will take you where you want to go. When you finally get to your destination, you are screened by the receptionist, intimidated by an efficient secretary, and then permitted to cool your heels and contemplate your guilt. I always feel that I am intruding on someone's very important schedule [Field notes].

The PMHA is located on the fourth floor of this building, down the hall from the State Mental Health suite. The top floor houses the Metropolitan Services Council and the United Fund office. On the mezzanine, there are conference rooms shared by all agencies; and on the ground floor is a large cafeteria used for coffee breaks, lunches, and off stage conversations.

As an off stage area, the cafeteria provides an excellent vantage point for the observation of status systems, unofficial communication channels, and dietary habits of agency personnel. The most democratic time of day is early morning. It is then that all of the people who don't eat breakfast at home congregate for a quick cup of coffee and a brief discussion of headlines. Since the working day has not officially begun, or perhaps because coffee has become a secular sacrament, rank is transcended as clerical workers and top executives share tables and comments; at all other times, secretaries eat with their peers.

At 9:20, well ahead of the crowd, the Metropolitan Services Council staff arrives and pre-empts the double table nearest the coffee dispenser. Like United Fund personnel, members of this agency remain segregated, cordial but not particularly hospitable to table hoppers. Smaller agencies mix freely, unless, as often happens, the cafeteria is used for an informal staff meeting.

Early arriving volunteers are often critical of the coffee ritual. But in many instances, the informal conversation provides an opportunity for the exchange of information which could not be transmitted through regular channels or in the presence of secretaries.

At lunch time, when volunteers are present, conversations become more guarded and exchange of backstage secrets or gossip about the most recent United Fund edict is postponed.

Who is having an important meeting on any given day can be deduced from the sharply creased trousers or the freshly coiffed hair. With these exceptions, the overall impression of costuming is one of cautious respectability.

The PMHA Setting

In the agency headquarters, although individual actors may have personal settings—an office, a desk, or a niche—these personal settings are a part of the shared scenic background. Thus, the practical joker who tacks the sign "Thimk" to the wall behind his desk may be a source of irritation to a co-worker who dislikes being defined as the kind of person who works in an office decorated with whimsical signs.

Except for several of these touches of "humor," a moribund philodendron, and four wall plaques attesting to the agency's public relations acumen, office decor is undistinguished utilitarian. Asphalt tile floors, walls painted institutional green, bare windows, and the inevitable clutter of overcrowded workspace, attest to the fact that United Fund money is not squandered on frills. (The only offices which have carpeting and drapes are those where wealthy auxiliaries have provided the scenic equipment.)

The office arrangement of the PMHA permits little privacy. Since there is no foyer or waiting room, entrance is into a common area occupied by secretaries, volunteer clerical workers, and visitors. The latter may be clients of the psychiatric social worker—ambulatory schizophrenics, emotionally disturbed "walk-ins," or ex-patients with rehabilitation problems. But visitors may also be Board members, salesmen, typewriter repairmen, or visiting dignitaries. Professional staff members work in six by six foot windowed cubicles with three-quarter walls, except for the social worker whose special need for confidentiality requires full wall partitions and opaque glass.

In the common room and its cubicles, an audience is nearly always present and audience segregation is almost impossible. One employee, in an attempt to make her office a backstage retreat, plastered cubicle windows with mental health posters, but quickly learned that her closed door was considered symptomatic of antisocial behavior. Even when visual barriers are successfully employed, the thin partitions permit offstage conversations only when the clatter of office machinery is loud enough to mute the words of the conversants. Thus, a mimeograph stopped in mid-sentence may shatter a fostered impression.

The Executive Director's office provides a little more latitude. It is an area about ten by eighteen feet, with full partitions and no glass, separated from the rest of the office and equipped with vinyl upholstered furniture symbolic of his differentiated status.

In this room, the rigid decorum of the outer office may be relaxed, and in the absence of outsiders, backstage language is frequently used. Here, the descriptive terms, "emotionally disturbed" or "mentally ill," are replaced by "all screwed up," "nutty as a fruitcake," "schizzy as hell," or "way out in left field." However, in staff conversations such usages are usually confined to descriptions of absent volunteers or present employees, and are rarely employed in reference to patients. By contrast, formal terms are used facetiously. In staff repartee, an individual expressing a complaint may receive the response, "Oh, you're just paranoid," while an off-color remark may evoke, "Your superego is mighty loose today."

Even here, however, the thinness of the walls must be respected, and the Executive habitually talks so low that even the most mundane conversation has a conspiratorial tone. Until they become accustomed, most new employees and volunteers tend to fear their hearing is failing. One volunteer said:

> He always seems to be letting you in on a big secret, but I never hear him well enough to find out what the secret is. I always wonder what I've said 'Yes' to [Field notes].

Desk Decorum

That the appearance of the office fosters an unfavorable impression is a matter of periodic concern to the Executive. In addition to the clutter produced by the large volume of mimeographed material and mailings, professional staff members frequently work with several committees simultaneously and have desks stacked with lists, folders, literature, etc. Since reprimands in regard to neatness tend to provoke hostile responses, the Executive attempts to cope with the situation by issuing memos or leaving terse notes on the offenders' desks.

The amount of desk decorum demanded is generally related to the personality or the profession of the current President of the Board. During the tenure of an authoritarian business executive, Board Meeting days were preceded by extensive tidying. When a media executive held the office, it was not considered necessary to bare the desktop, however, clutter was arranged in orderly stacks. If clergy occupy the top spot, neatness of desk tends to be replaced by decorum in dress, and female employees take special pains to appear wholesome. "But the toughest one of all," a former staff member said, "was when we had the University Dean and we all tried to look intellectual" (Field notes).

7
SUSTAINING THE COLLECTIVE IMAGE

Although the office setting may be inconvenient or incongruous in relation to an idealized definition of the situation, for the actors it possesses the advantages of known and fixed qualities. The real complexities of the dramatic interaction arise from the fact that the office walls provide the boundaries of an activity system in which personal fronts must be integrated into a collective front capable of sustaining a relevant image before ever-changing audiences.

For each performer, appearance and manner are the essential components for his personal front—that is, the impression of the role self which he fosters in making his claim to certain responses. In his presentation of self, all others, including his teammates, are his audience. However, whether or not he cooperates with others to sustain the imagery, his personal front becomes a part of a collective front. Further, there is a reciprocal relationship between the two: the personal front of each individual within the activity system helps define, and is to some extent defined by the fronts of all other individuals. When all of the personal fronts are consistent with role expectations, when cooperative efforts are successful in fostering an idealized image, the status of each individual is enhanced—a fact which may partially explain George Homans' suggestion (1950: 117) that "the warmth of feeling between companions may be vastly heightened by their joint and successful confrontation of a dangerous environment." By the same token, the individual whose appearance and manner deviate from accepted norms discredits the collectivity, decreases its opportunities for success, and diminishes the status of his colleagues.

Normative Expectations

The normative expectations for anyone who is a part of the United Fund bureaucracy require a personal front which conveys an impression of wholesomeness and dedication.

Although the wholesome look does not require a female employee to conform to the ancient stereotype of the social worker—i.e., sensible shoes, practical hair-do, and the slightly outmoded dark blue dress or suit—it is the general observation that high style is a prerogative of the volunteer. As a member of the supporting cast, the Good Samaritan Foundation performer is expected not to outshine the leading lady. An elaborate hair style or avant garde fashion is generally the mark of a new employee. Whether these individuals terminate employment (probably) or become invisible by conformity (possibly) is a matter of conjecture. However, the sanction which effects their disappearance is a ribald type of kidding directed at both the employee and her employer.

The requirements for men are comparable. Male staff members or executives do not grow beards, wear love beads, nor affect the sartorial splendor of men of distinction. The individual, whatever his personal taste or life style may be, is expected to have the conservative appearance of one to whom the wise use of the donor dollar may be entrusted.

The Dedicated Look

The imagery of dedication is also considered to be reassuring to benefactors. Since the word carries the connotation of working more for love than for money, the person who can convey the impression of a commitment above and beyond the call of duty is considered an excellent personnel investment. While the term is used descriptively as an accolade, some staff members do not consider it complimentary. One observed, "When they start calling you 'dedicated' it's time to ask for a raise. You can be sure you are overworked and underpaid." When a staff member begins to resist this expectation, he may be expressing disaffection for the performance and also for his role as dedicated cynic. While he may still believe in the sacred nature of the mission, he has begun to question the morality of the means.

The opprobrium which some professionals attach to this term was described by Edward D. Greenwood, M.D., Co-Director of School Mental Health for the Menninger Foundation, and also a Deputy Director of the Joint Commission on Mental Health of Children. In Pangloss to evaluate a Mental Health Conference, he observed:

> Dedication connotes a sentimental rather than a professional approach. As an immediate example, take the fellow who just said: "Isn't it heartwarming that so many people are interested in Mental Health! Isn't it wonderful that they'll even give up their Saturday for our conference!"
>
> Is this truly a *measure* of your meeting? Frankly, I have some concern for the mental health of your 700 participants. On a beautiful autumn day like this, they might be better off at a football game [Field notes].

A second observer, the executive of a treatment facility with a rigorous research program, said:

> Committed to doing a damn interesting job, yes; but 'dedicated'—no. This is the type who says, 'If I only have helped one little child, my ten years' work are all worthwhile.' Believe me, anytime you have a person who can be gratified with such meager results, you have a person who is incapable of honest evaluation [Field notes].

The tension between the values of activity-justified-by-success and activity-validated-by-research is a source of conflict. The normative expectation that a person should be visibly engaged in furthering the cause is both action and future oriented. An Education Director said:

> Here, evaluation consists of sitting around and recounting the compliments. Anybody who is reported to have complained about a program is simply labeled a troublemaker. When we do go through the motions of providing participants with evaluation forms, nothing is ever done with them. A staff member who insists on evaluation is told: 'There's no time to sit around studying what's past—we've got to forge ahead!'
> Frankly, I think honest evaluation is too threatening. If we found out what we're really accomplishing, we'd probably all commit hari-kari [Field notes].

Role Strain

The expectation of unwavering dedication is one which creates considerable strain in maintaining the personal front, and is also one of the greatest sources of hostility between staff and volunteers.

Because he receives no remuneration, the volunteer views his contribution as sacrificial. Staff is well aware of his sacrifice. But volunteers do not recognize that *most staff members contribute more "volunteer" hours than volunteers do.* Staff's 37½ hour work week is real only in terms of salary. And the stipulation that "overtime worked in units of four hours or more shall be compensated by equal time off" (Pangloss County Board Manual) is rarely observed. The consensus of professional staff was expressed by one who said:

> Volunteers are so used to letting somebody else do the dirty work that they never think about how many overtime hours go into putting on one of these public affairs. Yet they expect you to look bright, cheerful, and delighted to fetch one more brief case or carry three more chairs. Only once did I ever tell a Board President I was tired . . . he said, 'Look doll, getting tired is what you get paid for' [Field notes].

Such expressions of resentment are not unusual. In a society where money is a measure of a man's worth, that which is free is often considered worthless. The individual who works for nothing is secure to the extent that others, also working for nothing, reaffirm the value of such action. However, with the formalization of social action, the mixture of paid professionals and unpaid volunteers provides the basis for invidious comparisons and dissonance.

Role Distance

Sustaining the dedicated front presents special problems to the staff member in charge of publicity. Since most agency publicists are ex-newspaper reporters, they have been previously socialized to the normative requirements of the professional journalist. Hence, their reference group remains the Fourth Estate, even though their membership group is agency personnel.

In journalism, sentimental dedication is not a particularly valued characteristic—except, perhaps, for the lovelorn editor. Instead, expectations are for ingenuity, honesty, aggressiveness accuracy, and some degree of literacy. When a reporter becomes a press agent, these role expectations change only slightly. As an overt partisan of a special interest, he is expected to exaggerate the importance of the interest he represents; but he is nonetheless expected to retain his integrity in dealing with facts.

My own experience as a participant in this process was that of role conflict. Initially, in working with the agency as a freelance publicist for the Christmas project, my role was peripheral. Since I had no intimate contact with the mechanics of the performance, developing news stories with honest enthusiasm was completely consistent with journalistic norms. However, in the years when I was responsible for both the performance and the publicity, knowledge of the discrepancies between what was and what was professed became a handicap and source of discomfort.

Publicists for other agencies describe similar difficulties. Committed to the norms of their membership group, but attached to the norms of the reference group, they tend to resist the dominant values of the United Fund agencies. Further, they frequently become friends with colleagues in other agencies who occupy similar marginal roles and these relationships are characterized by supportive encounters in which the self presented denies the self implied by the occupational role (Goffman, 1961: 105-132).

One such friendship group met together with irregular frequency over a period of several years. By lunching at the Press Club, a private restaurant restricted to media people, the participants enjoyed the double advantage of the proximity of the reference group while maintaining the maximum social distance from their agency co-workers.

Although these sessions became an elaborate parody of the absurdities of their situated roles—a kind of black mass intended to profane the sacred—the profanation was primarily restricted to the areas of discrepancy between the normative expectations of reference group and membership group. Volunteers in general and executives in particular were avoided subjects, but the system itself was ridiculed through the construction of incongruous fantasies.

Thus, the interagency trio became a team of performers engaged in presenting a private performance for their own benefit—a fact which they duly acknowledged by calling their encounters "benefit luncheons." At their first meeting, having agreed with mock gravity that "proper structure implements objectives," they rejected an election of officers on the grounds that each person would undoubtedly vote for himself, but did decide that they should have a name and an objective. The suggestion finally accepted was the Anti-Semantic Society—an organization dedicated to stamping out social work jargon. Defined as dirty words were all the cliches of social uplift, with special penalties assigned to "per se," "heartwarming," "meaningful," "enthusiastic efforts," and "it is believed that . . . ."

One of the favorite diversions of the group was the fabrication of "agencies-I'd-like-to-direct." It was generally agreed that the job which would offer the most-least for the executive would be a Society for the Prevention of Impoverished Physicians; while the most needed—especially during the season of televised pro football—was a Home for Married Mothers, with the promotional slogan, "You can get further farther from father." The most elaborate imaginary agency was not originated within the group, but by a group member while he was attending a training session for respiratory disease employees. He described it as follows:

> Somebody read a paper about a disease discovered up in Nova Scotia. It had first been noticed among agricultural workers exposed to the spore of a fungus that grows on fodder. They called it "Farmer's Lung."
>
> We were sitting around in the bar that night and somebody mentioned that it was a damn shame this disease was so obscure, and we decided it needed promoting. So, we organized. We called ourselves the Fodderated Farmer's Lung and Health Association, with headquarters in Lung Island. Our trademark was a double-barred lung, and our mascot a cow—in dung-arees, of course. But the real genius was in our promotion plans. Since the incidence of Farmer's Lung was only six, we figured we could both raise money and spread the disease by selling Christmas seals with mucilage impregnated with fungus spores [Field notes].

If the P.R. person attempts to use humor as a means of disclaiming the "phony" aspects of his role, there are other staff members who try to remove themselves from those aspects which are discreditably real.

The professional pariah, in exploiting his outcast status, is fully aware that his stigma makes others apprehensive. To reassure them that his former role of mental patient has been completely discarded, he attempts to present a self which is super-normal. One means of becoming a hero of adjustment is to laugh at those things which others fear. By telling the stereotype-reinforcing jokes which his co-workers suppress, the pariah removes himself from the category of those whose sickness entitles them to special consideration. When the PMHA asked for suggestions for a name for the student volunteer organization, it was the pariahs who suggested "Psycho-Pals," "Schizoteenic," "TeeNuts," and "Booby-Soxers" (Field notes).

Such humor is also a characteristic of people who work in agencies furthering causes which are "not quite respectable." Although Planned Parenthood is staffed by people who are True Believers, it has also been a prolific source of birth control jokes. However, this staff humor reflects an interesting change in public attitudes. In 1960, the favorite joke was about the old maid from St. Paul, who went to the Birth Control Ball, bought all the devices at fabulous prices and nobody asked her at all. In 1967, the story most widely circulated concerned the Catholic woman who wistfully observed that she really didn't care whether the Pope gave them the red light or the green light; it was the flashing amber that was making her nervous.

Another example of such humor was displayed by social workers attached to a center for the prevention of venereal diseases who referred to their place of employment as "The Clap-Trap." Their suggested slogan: "Through these doors pass the most cultured girls in the world—cultured three times a week" (Field notes).

In all of these examples, humor was a mechanism for reducing the tensions generated when the role-self is not consistent with the definition of ideal self which the performer desires to project. Desacralization provides a means of disclaiming discrepant aspects of a role.

EXPRESSIVE CONTROL

The employee who denies discrepant aspects of his role defines more than self. Although sustaining a collective front is a team effort, any individual is a team performer on any occasion when he does a solo routine in which absent teammates are dependent upon his action for a revelant definition of the situation.

In this context, the way in which the Executive Director exercises his authority is perceived as definitive of the normative expectations of the Board of Directors. Or, a secretary, alone in the office, may be considered a team performer insofar as her performance is perceived as representative of the agency.

Thus, every performance communicates information at several levels. At the interpersonal level, the individual stages a performance in which all others are the audience. At the team, or group level, he cooperates in presenting routines designed for co-workers and outsiders; and at the collectivity level, he helps to convey a collective image to the society which comprises the environment.

Since the maintenance of expressive control is primarily contingent upon shared information and audience segregation, when there exists a working consensus on the professed definition of the situation, when all performers know and accept the norms governing the situation, and when the performance is staged before a single, known audience, conditions are favorable for the control of discrepant information.

However, there are complicating factors. Each of the three levels of rank—the executive, the associate, and the secretarial—permits a different amount and kind of privileged information. Since clerical employees are supposed to believe that the professed reality is the real reality, norms which determine the subtle adjustment of imagery are often left unstated, and inappropriate behavior is not defined until after-the-fact by the institution of punitive sanctions.

In its broadest sense, the professed definition of the situation is as follows:

(1) The Mental Health Association provides more service for each United Fund Dollar than any other agency.
(2) Each employee works continuously, efficiently, and harmoniously with all other employees in support of the efforts of enthusiastic volunteers.
(3) Every volunteer is a *Very Important Person* whose contribution, no matter how small, is vitally needed and deeply appreciated. The Association will provide him the most satisfaction for the least effort.

Since wages constitute a source of dissonance for volunteers, the fact that employees are paid money for their dedication is regarded as discreditable information which ought to be concealed. Since real concealment is an obvious impossibility, United Fund contributions are solicited to provide "services" rather than to pay salaries. What makes this semantic manipulation particularly interesting is that it provides the convolution of logic through which all agency activity becomes, by definition, "service." Thus, it necessarily follows that the more active the employee appears, the more service he is appearing to provide.

In the Mental Health Association, the appearance of being busy requires no deception. The agency is continuously engaged in the implementation of projects designed to be the "biggest," "the most unique," or "the most important" service ever offered the community. Moreover, frequent changes of personnel result in perpetual understaffing. Even when replacements are immediately available, the probability is high that at any given time someone will be either leaving or learning, and thus inadequately filling a role.

The work load of professional staff requires that coffee breaks and lunches be frequently missed, or used as an out-of-the-office opportunity for uninterrupted continuation of work. Overtime (unpaid) is the norm; deadline jitters are commonplace; and the executive, in attempting to exercise his directive dominance, moves about the office, head thrust forward, shoulders hunched, in the semi-erect posture of one who is literally plunging from one activity to another.

If the habitual pace is described by the staff as "hectic," outside observers tend to use different adjectives. By other Good Samaritan Foundation agency personnel, the office is described as "frantic." Some Board members call it "dedicated," but others appear to perceive the activity as too aggressive. One Board member commented:

> Nobody expects such heroic efforts. You all act as if you expected to change the world over night, and you can't. Anybody who works like you do just has to be neurotic [Field notes].

The Executive Director appears to regard all such feedback as complimentary—evidence that the organization is effectively conveying an impression of vigor.

But if the busy appearance requires no deception, the impression of harmonious cooperation requires a great deal. What one employee described as "the cumulative crises" result in polar types of interaction. With the buildup of stress, relationships become increasingly strained and status differentiation is exaggerated. Requests become commands, and the reaction is often a mocking display of deference. In such periods of tension, the priority of mimeograph use can precipitate conflict in which the loser defines defeat as a threatening dispossession of status.

On the other hand, when it appears that everything which possibly can go wrong has, tension release can become near hysteria. Interaction is characterized by familiarity, laughter, and a general lack of restraint.

Since interaction is so often at one extreme or the other, "normal" activity must be replaced by a more formal decorum in the presence of outsiders. When a volunteer is present, the appropriate front is one of deference. Secretaries defer to the professional staff, professionals defer to the Executive, and everyone defers to the volunteer. If the visitor is from the United Fund office, a similar front is employed except that courtesy is substituted for deference. The difference is subtle, but important. By the differentiation, the agency acknowledges a symbiotic relationship, but at the same time affirms its own autonomy.

The greatest problem lies in knowing which collective front is required. A relatively high turnover in clerical staff results in employees who are many times unable to distinguish between a prospective patient and a potential benefactor; moreover, their status denies them specific knowledge of the reasons for the differentiation. In addition, neither the Director nor the Associates know all of the volunteers working on all committees.

To cue-in teammates on which front should be in effect requires that everyone be alert to the on-stage presence of any outsider and that he be identified as quickly as possible by name and activity. Thus, a typical greeting by the staff member in the know is a loud and clear "Hello, Mrs. *Smith*, are you here for the *Board* meeting?" Or, to a United Fund staff member, "Hi Hank, how are things *upstairs*?" If other staff members need not have been expected to recognize the intruder, introductions are in order all around.

111

Since calling a volunteer by name is considered essential to making his volunteer experience meaningful, staff members take great pains to link names and faces. If memory fails, the deference front must be cued-in by a warm and effusive greeting. Obviously if the outsider has an affluent or pre-possessing look, the deference front is automatic. However, if he looks disreputable, he is *never* asked if he wants to see the psychiatric social worker. *To mistake a benefactor for a patient is an unforgivable faux pas.*

In instances where status differentiation precludes the sharing of full information, loyalty is often effective in sustaining the imagery in a subordinate-superordinate team performance. Thus, a secretary, not knowing whether her supervisor wants to become involved in a telephone conversation with a given volunteer, may say: "I think she's out, but let me check." Since secretarial importance is enhanced by the supervisor's importance, a loyal secretary often exaggerates creditable information and conceals that which is discreditable. For example, "out for coffee" is translated as "in conference at the moment"—a statement which is frequently no lie. When a volunteer comes into the office, phone calls for the involved staff member are usually held. "Setting up the volunteer," or "giving him the VIP treatment," are backstage terms describing the fostered impression that this volunteer among all volunteers is special. Hence, it is considered tactful to protect him from hearing staff fostering a similar impression (via telephone) to another volunteer. Or, as Goffman (1959: 49-51) has observed, one avoids exposing the line as a standard routine.

It is also possible for a member of the clerical staff who wishes to be subversive to destroy a fostered impression by a too literal transmission of truth. In one such instance, a loner on the secretarial staff was resentful of her exclusion from staff conferences. Therefore, in intercepting calls to Associate Directors, she managed to convey an ambiguous impression by stating dramatically: "She can't come to the phone right now. *She's behind closed doors with Mr._____*." The practice was not revealed until she mistook a staff member's husband for a member of the Board.

8
PERFORMANCE ROUTINES AND RITUALS

Although the agency's imagery is designed to imply that staff works in support of volunteers' enthusiastic efforts, in reality, a great portion of staff energy is directed to overcoming apathy. Therefore, the development of an acceptable program requires that it have high volunteer appeal, good publicity potential, and some means for involving a large or important segment of the community.

Once such a program has been constructed, the selection of a chairman is partially determined by the kind of virtue which needs to be dramatized, and partially by the availability of the right volunteer. For most programs, the ideal chairman is a "name brand" peripheral pariah; however, since these two attributes are infrequently combined, the usual choice is the socially prominent career volunteer. To reinforce the impression that the agency is democratic in its development of community leadership—and especially when no preferable alternative is available—a socially acceptable unknown may be chosen. To meet the acceptability criteria for the community-wide project, the General Chairman (during the time period of this study) was generally a white upper middle class Protestant. (Negroes were offered less visible posts on advisory committees and the Board of Directors.)

In the event that a volunteer is unknown, it is considered a public relations essential that he have an interesting background (e.g., Rhodes scholar, lady pilot, lighthouse keeper) or a fascinating hobby (e.g., harpsichord building, skin diving, or gourmet cooking) which may be exploited in the necessary "puff job"—a backstage term with no official counterpart which refers to the publicity buildup necessary to create a newsworthy personality.

Socializing the Chairman

When the tentative selection has been made, there must be a decision on which agency approach will be the most effective in securing the volunteer's acceptance. If the selectee is prominent and his participation is considered vitally important, the invitation is issued by the Executive, with the project director in a supportive role. Whether this is handled by telephone, by an expense account luncheon, or by a request to "come-down-to-the-office, we-need-to-get-your-advice," depends entirely upon an intuitive assessment of the volunteer's receptivity to any given approach.

If it is apparent that his concept of involvement consists of little more than name lending, or if he is a "discovery" who is not sure what will be expected, a completed staff plan, neatly typed in outline form, is submitted to him at the initial meeting as "some ideas you might like to consider and do feel free to make any changes." If he accepts it in its entirety, he is asked for recommendations of personnel for his committee. Since he is probably unprepared to make these recommendations, staff produces a list of "people-you-might-enjoy-working-with." By this time, the new chairman, outnumbered two to one and reassured by the efficiency—"You people have thought of everything!"—acquiesces to the well-planned importunings of his seducers.

If he is an initiate, he usually appears relieved that he will not be expected to produce a brilliant plan of his own; at the same time, he seems to feel vaguely uneasy. Aware of the nature of his doubts, staff members review the "marvelous ideas" he has contributed and remind him that this will be truly one of the most important projects the Association has ever undertaken. He is assured, "You don't need to worry about anything. We'll keep in touch." And with important business completed, the staff implementor is then ready to ghost-write the presidential letter of appointment.

Although name lenders may be of either sex, the "working volunteer" is more often a woman. For her, the initiation technique is somewhat different. The staff plan is left open-ended, and wherever possible she is given the opportunity to make choices between equally desirable alternatives, or sometimes between alternatives which are obviously unequal. However, here too there is the helpful guidance of staff.

The typical working chairman appears to feel that her worth derives from the fact that she makes staff work easier. This is not the case. Except in complex programs involving hundreds of volunteers (e.g., the Christmas program) the active participation of a chairman greatly increases the expenditure of staff time and energy. The necessity of frequent consultations, additional meetings, adjustments of schedule to allow for her bridge dates, golf games, and baby sitter problems, all become complicating factors. However, in spite of the frustrations and extra work, this volunteer is highly valued. Her working knowledge of the program not only makes her a reliable teammate, but more important, her participation gives the program authenticity. With real involvement on the part of the volunteer, there is less destructive information to conceal and relationships can be honest.

The Kick-Off Meeting

Whether a volunteer is a name lender or a worker, mutual expectations of role relationships are established by the time of the Kick-Off meeting. This is the assembling of the committee who, in the agency cliche, "will carry the ball."

In passing, it should be noted that at this stage the military terminology—i.e., "the battle for . . . ," "the crusade against . . . ," is replaced by the idiom of the game. It is also noteworthy that within this framework, those who join the team are recruited not so much for their scrimmage ability as for the luster they will add to the booster section. The chairman, therefore, must be half evangelist, half cheerleader. He must be able to say, with the religious fervor, "The theme for the year is Go! Go! Go!"

Like the love feast, or agapé of the early Christians, the Kick-Off meeting begins with a ceremonial meal hopefully designed to induce a mood of benevolent enthusiasm. Whether it be breakfast, luncheon, dinner, or banquet, the most favorable settings for fostering an impression of a momentous occasion, are, in descending order:(1) a prestige private club, (2) a major hotel, (3) a catered luncheon in the agency building, or (4) the last resort—a Dutch treat carry-your-own-tray type lunch featuring Good Samaritan Foundation cuisine.

For the agency, the first setting represents a kind of coming-of-age in Pangloss. Since agency budgets do not permit private club prices, a luncheon in this setting carries a clear implication of establishment patronage. At the other end of the scale, the tray lunch, while lacking in prestige, can be turned into a public relations victory. It fosters the image of loyal volunteers engaged in a sacrificial rite.

The objective of the Kick-Off Meeting is to launch a program, campaign, or project by capturing the volunteer's interest, securing from him some kind of commitment, and giving him a sense of participation. Thus, the setting requires careful attention to all details which might endanger rather than engender enthusiasm.

Since an empty chair is equated with apostasy or lack of interest, the R.S.V.P. and telephone followup are devices used to insure an occupant for every seat. Moreover, if a choice must be made, the preferred room is the one which is just a trifle too small. An overflow crowd increases the feeling of intimacy and contributes to emotional contagion. To emphasize the import of the project, and the expectation of participation, such properties as information packets, note paper, and sharpened pencils are arranged with geometric precision by each place setting.

The Rituals

Opening ceremonies are planned to establish a Gemeinschaft warmth, and to impress guests with the prestige of their peers. If the meeting is held in a private club or hotel, the bartender often provides an unwitting assist in the establishment of fellowship and conviviality. However, the customary procedure tends to place the responsibility on the Chairman. If the meeting is not too large, all guests are individually introduced and clearly identified as persons capable of important contributions.

The second part of the performance is the ritual of inspiration. If the Chairman is dynamic and charismatic, he may be permitted to handle the role alone—with, of course, the guidance of the ubiquitous idiot sheet. However, it is often necessary that his performance be reinforced by professional enthusiasts who add lustre and legitimacy by their glowing endorsements of the project. With a low-budget operation, these may be local celebrities—television or political personalities; or in the health field, a wellknown doctor or professional pariah. Staff members remain in the background, frequently in the role of resource persons.

Having established what the proposed program will do for the community, the next step is to determine what the volunteers will do for the program. This is the crucial moment of audience participation which can make or break a project. If the first response is hesitant, cautious, or negative, the agency's investment in enthusiasm will be irretrievably lost, along with considerable loss of face.

Engineered Spontaneity

That this type of disaster is forestalled may be credited to staff's foresight in planting a confederate in the audience who, on cue, springs to his feet and without waiting for recognition from the chair dramatically provides an instant pledge. What he pledges depends upon whether the association is asking for funds, gifts, volunteers, or program reservations. And whether this pledge is ever honored is unimportant. Its value lies in setting the pace; it indicates the level at which the bid for status will be successful.

At this point, expectations established during the introduction ritual produce predictable results. Since each participant has been previously identified as a mover and shaker, he can live up to his role requirements only by outbidding his coparticipants. If he fails, it is he, not the agency, who loses face.

Such engineered spontaneity is a near universal practice among the more aggressive agencies—but it is also to be observed in one form or another at church, PTA, or even faculty meetings. It is arranged with relative ease. It requires only that staff find one volunteer who may be safely entrusted with the confederate role. The usual approach is:

> What we need is someone with your influence and enthusiasm to be a kind of pace-setter. If people know that you—and your organization—are supporting us, we can really put this thing over. Do you think you could possibly be ready to make a firm commitment of, say 500, at Friday's meeting? [Field notes].

In some cases, only one audience confederate is necessary; in others, competitive shills are set up by strategic "leaks" of information. One organization, in a massive volunteer recruitment effort, managed to create an intense competition between women's church groups. When the Catholic diocesan representative agreed to be the pace setter, advance information was "leaked" to Protestant and Jewish groups. In this particular situation, the engineered enthusiasm became unexpectedly genuine when the interfaith competition was eclipsed by a battle of the sexes. As each church representative was attempting to out-witness the others, a Union executive, addressing himself to the male contingent, said:

> Now fellows, we can't let these little ladies do all the work. I can pledge the cooperation of our 2,500 service representatives. How about you? [Field notes].

Sustaining Enthusiasm

It is well known to staff that the witness of faith and pledges of good works evoked in the revival-like atmosphere of the Kick-Off meeting cannot be considered firm. Unless there is extensive followup, the majority of the converts become backsliders. To provide such followup requires that a large amount of staff time be devoted to reinforcing the volunteer's image of himself as a vitally important wheel in the operation. He is praised for every effort, no matter how ineffective; his telephone calls are always welcomed, no matter how inopportune. One staff member said:

> Actually, I am able to control less than 10% of my time—the rest is spent talking to volunteers. Some you have to push every step of the way, and others are so enthusiastic that they call to report each success. If a volunteer is giving top priority to a project, he naturally expects staff to do the same. There is just no tactful way to tell him that you are also involved in other important projects [Field notes].

The Planning Session

A second kind of luncheon meeting is the planning session. This may involve a relatively small number of people in a general meeting, or it may be a large affair which begins with the inspirational format of the Kick-Off, after which subcommittees separate for workshop sessions. The latter arrangement is considered conducive to increased interaction and thus a greater sense of participation and involvement. However, one volunteer described her experiences with a respiratory disease agency as follows:

It was my first meeting and I didn't know much about the disease. At lunch, I sat between two very dedicated ladies who discussed sputum all through the salad course. As soon as I went to the workshop, somebody appointed me recorder and I was miserable—trying to spell medical terms I couldn't even pronounce, and trying to find out who moved what.

When it was over and I was sitting there wondering how I'd ever make sense out of my muddled notes, some staff woman came up and literally snatched them out of my hand. I asked her to please give me a chance to get them in order. But she said—very condescendingly, I thought—"Oh I'm used to volunteer's notes. I wouldn't think of letting you write them up. That's what staff is for!"

A week later, I got a neat mimeographed copy of "my" minutes—describing things I couldn't even remember happening. I was amazed. And then it hit me! That's why they had that tape recorder there [Field notes].

The contrived sense of participation is rarely so obvious, and few staff members are so heavy-handed in fostering the impression of enthusiastic support. However, the planning session frequently provides volunteers little more than an opportunity to acquiesce to a completed staff plan. In most cases, the ability to make any but a superficial contribution is limited by the volunteer's circumstances: he has had no opportunity to examine the proposal in advance, to think through its possible consequences, or to consider other alternatives. Moreover, he has a natural reluctance to appear over-critical and he is also aware that an in-depth discussion will prolong the meeting.

123

Predictable Interaction

In such a meeting, the largest part—and always some part—of the interaction is completely spontaneous and yet almost without variation. The opening statement, "What we really need is good publicity!" is made in the tone of one reaffirming a major social value which others have forgotten. The response is enthusiastic:

> How about contacting the weeklies? I know the editor of the *Fireside Topics* . . .
>
> Maybe we can get somebody on the "Crucial Issues" show. . .
> My sister lives next door to a fellow who works at the Gazette [Field notes].

For staff, this is another moment when expressive control is subjected to excessive strain. An efficient agency has well established and complex relationships with media. To get good publicity, the P.R. man must promise exclusive stories to the major dailies; to maintain good relations, exclusives must be awarded with absolute impartiality. The P.R. person lives in the fear of offending an editor, of losing his reputation as a "right guy"—which means that he must be professionally accurate, uncomplaining, and aware enough of schedules to keep out of the city room at deadline time.

The saving grace in this situation is that the volunteer's eagerness to help on publicity tends to die very quickly when he contemplates the actual writing of a press release. Therefore, the agency can maintain its control of information with a gracious, noncommittal assurance to the volunteer that his offer will certainly be remembered in the event that difficulties are encountered.

Special Effects

It also seems to be a truism that while volunteers believe that good publicity solves all problems, few ever read it. Several agencies have learned that the appearance of good press coverage is almost as effective as the reality. Like many dramaturgical devices, this is a chance discovery. In one case, an agency, which had inadvertently scheduled a meeting at a time when all media personnel were engaged elsewhere, hired an off-duty news photographer to take pictures of all the ceremonies so that acceptable photos could accompany its own news releases. Although none of these pictures was ever used, volunteer praise for "the wonderful press coverage" was effusive. As a result, the photographer and his flashbulbs are employed to foster the impression of newsmaking at every agency function. For a conference, this cost can run well over one-hundred United Fund dollars.

When media coverage is available, the staff public relations director is sometimes placed in the awkward position of judging relative importance of volunteers by selecting the "no-more-than-five" subjects for a group photo. Since this is one of the few sanctions that a staff person can exercise, it must be used to full advantage. If the P.R. person has a good working relationship with the press, it is sometimes possible to make a side arrangement whereby the photographer is commissioned to take a second shot at the agency's expense. Thus, twice as many volunteers can win the recognition of being newsworthy. The volunteers whose picture does not get published are encouraged to blame the photo editor.

A second technique is sometimes employed when courtesy to minor dignitaries requires their inclusion in a picture at the expense of the volunteers. In such a case, which also involves collusion between press and agency, the five volunteers are posed in the center with the dignitaries in flanking positions. When the picture is developed, cropping eliminates the dignitaries—but once again, the omission cannot be blamed on the agency.

Fostering the Impression of Gratitude

Publicity is only one avenue by which an agency can demonstrate recognition and appreciation for a volunteer's efforts. Actually, the expression of gratitude constitutes a whole field of agency activity.

For some organizations, the posting of volunteer hours requires extensive bookkeeping; and the agency which does not properly recognize volunteer contributions with awards, pins, certificates, plaques, and appreciation ceremonies is considered guilty of a moral lapse.

In the Mental Health Christmas program, it is not unusual for committee chairmen to receive five thank-you letters. The first is the mimeographed acknowledgement sent to all contributors; the second, a typewritten letter from the agency executive or Board President; the third, an agency originated letter over the signature of the general chairman; fourth, a letter from the hospital superintendent in behalf of the patients; and finally, a personal note from the professional staff project director. In addition, there is a public thank-you in the Association newsletter. In most cases, all letters (except the hospital's) are written by the same individual—an onerous task of devising new variations of old cliches. A public relations director, saddled with the appreciation amenities in another agency, said: "There are lots of cases where the dollar and cents cost of staff time is greater than the value of contribution. The whole damn bit has gotten out of hand" (Field notes).

126

Although there is volunteer criticism of the agency which is remiss, the agency which overdoes its thank-yous is also censured. Of an organization which sent letters of appreciation to every United Fund contributor, a PMHA Board member said: "It's ridiculous. It must have cost well over $2,000. We'll soon need a second campaign to finance the gratitude" (Field notes).

9
SYMBIOTIC
COOPERATION

Up to this point our discussion has focused on the Association's efforts to sustain a definition of the situation which will evoke a cooperative response from volunteers. In such cases, the dramaturgy is directed to individuals who have voluntarily chosen to present themselves and who have made their choice from a wide variety of similar opportunities. Thus, the dramatic action is constructed with awareness of a buyer's market and the concomitant requirement of a competitive offering.

But the agency audience is not limited to volunteers. Its repertoire must also include acts designed to influence favorably those individuals who are more or less obligated to lend their support, and who, by fulfilling their obligations, can make reciprocal claims on the Association.

With United Fund affiliation, the agency becomes a part of an associational network. Within this network, symbiotic relationships require each participating association to help sustain a definition relevant to the financial success of the United Fund campaign. In this larger drama, just as each individual within an agency is dependent upon the cooperation of his coworkers in the task of sustaining a relevant collective front, so is each United Fund Affiliate dependent upon co-affiliates.

When the relationships are symbiotic, the dramatic inter-action is often a dialogue between cooperating teams from competing agencies. At the same time that each is engaged in imposing definitional claims upon the other, both are co-operatively involved in the projection of imagery which meets the expectations of their shared environment. But whether agency personnel play the part of actors or audience, co-operation in concealing discreditable information is contingent upon mutual benefits which are individually perceived.

The State Association

For the Pangloss Mental Health Association, the audience which is most permissive and supportive is the staff of the State Association for Mental Health. The physical proximity of the state office permits frequent interaction, and since there is neither rivalry nor the friction of work relationships, sentiments between staff members tend to be friendly. These staff members have reciprocal backstage privileges, and frequently they are not only aware of the dramaturgy, but have had a part in its construction. At a public performance, whichever staff is not on stage becomes an appreciative claque in the other's audience. The PMHA quota to the State Association is between forty and forty-five percent of its United Fund income.[1] Thus, the State organization has a vested interest in the success and continuing prosperity of the county chapter.

The United Fund

While the State Association plays the role of supported and supportive friend, the agency's relationship with the United Fund is characterized by the strain inherent in any situation where there are discrepant definitions. Although federated fund raising was initially defined as a service for the agencies and the community, the Association's delegation of this vital responsibility has been accompanied by a commensurate loss of autonomy.

The Association maintains the position that it is an autonomous organization whose programs, services, and objectives are properly the concern of its own citizens' Board of Directors. And further, it maintains privately (if not publicly) that the United Fund's interference in policy constitutes a usurpation of authority.

However, the economic interests which support the Fund justify its interference as necessary for the facilitation of rational organization. And with more than $5,000,000 of sanctioning power, it is the fund-raising arm which has the muscle. Hence, the United Fund's occupancy of the top floor of the Good Samaritan Foundation building is considered symbolic. In reference to its omnipotence, the backstage term for its executive is "The Man Upstairs."

Pressure for Status Quo

One of the more interesting as well as pressure generating activities of the funding agency is the evaluation of agency programs by its Board of Review. In determining whether an organization deserves increased or decreased support, one criterion of judgment is: "How *realistically* is the agency moving toward its goals?"[2] It is of particular significance here that although the question refers to *agency* goals, the actual evaluation is made on the basis of what the Fund considers to be "realistic." In relation to Mental Health, a Fund spokesman said:

> The professed goals and the philosophical position of the
> agency are irrelevant. Would you be disappointed if I told you
> that the real function of the Mental Health Association is to
> provide support to the people who are affected by this
> [mental illness] problem?[3]

Obviously, *providing support* for the victims of a social
problem is not the same as *effecting the social change* necessary
for the elimination of the problem. But it is safer. By preserving
the *status quo*, supportive services generate little opposition
which might decrease the flow of donor dollars and diminish
the success of the United Fund drive. Therefore, "realistically,"
the Mental Health Association—like many other philanthropy-
dependent social change organizations—is evaluated by how well
it supports the very system which produces the problems such
groups hope to solve.

The Fund spokesman explained further:

> A second criterion of evaluation is the agency's effectiveness in
> involving board members and volunteers in agency activities:
> for example, we look at attendance records at Board meetings.
> Anytime we find an agency which averages only a 15%
> attendance at meetings, that agency is in trouble [Field
> notes].

Granting that an agency which can muster only fifteen percent of its Board may well be in trouble, the position of the
Fund indicates that the emphasis is on *quantification*. What an
agency does is less important than how many are doing it. The
use of quantification as an evaluative index measures effectiveness in terms of mobilizing resources rather than in terms of
escalating action.

In regard to this second criterion, it is also noteworthy that this is an additional pressure for an agency to gear its activities to middle class volunteers rather than to lower class clients. The expectation that agencies will preserve the status quo makes controversial activity hazardous. Pangloss agency executives often quote the case of the agency head who was asked to resign because of his active support of an anti-establishment faction in a nonpartisan school board election. Hence, social action which might be considered controversial is either covert or forsworn. In the event that an agency executive expresses a nonconforming opinion, he is sure to add: "If you quote me, I'll say you lie."

Super Cooler and Competitor

The United Fund is a super-cooler. In insulating the community from the importunings of a multiplicity of fund-raisers, it, in effect, cools out the agency. For Mental Health, this means that the organization "which speaks for those who cannot speak for themselves" acquires a spokesman for its own needs. Thus, thrice-cooled—by the hospital, by the Association, and by the United Fund—the mental patient all but disappears into the social distance.

As an organization which is also competing for volunteers, the United Fund uses slogans which are subversive of affiliates' efforts: "Give once for All" has a double meaning which implies that nothing more will be expected. For the complacent American who does not take seriously his responsibility for democratic participation, the Fund is a source of comfort. Its rational calculation of what he can afford to have deducted from his pay check relieves him of responsibility. And the assurance that in contributing his "fair share" he is a "people helper" soothes him into believing that his contribution is adequate, Moreover, unless he is willing to ask embarrassing questions, he will be protected from the knowledge that his contribution is allocated on a discriminatory basis—e.g., there is no home in Pangloss for the unwed Negro mother, and at least one of the United Fund adoption agencies has never accepted a Negro child. Further, he may not realize that the United Fund "success" is anchored to an assessment of "what the traffic will bear" rather than to an evaluation of what the community needs.

The imagery of the Fund clearly implies that without its efforts, the sick, the halt, the lame, and the underprivileged would be destitute. On the basis of such an appeal, it imposes a quasi-taxation on the working class to help support middle class interests.

Loss of Identity

When the United Fund was inaugurated, to assure agencies that their identities would not be lost, and to assure donors that they could control the allocation of their donations, the funding organization agreed to provide space on the back of each pledge card with the notation: "If gift is to be designated to specific agency or agencies, please fill in name and pledge below." Since no agency has ever had designations exceeding its allocation, this is a device whose principal function is to satisfy a donor's desire to sanction.

However, the initial agreement in regard to designations is one which the Fund has come to regret. Although it results in no transferral of funds, it does obligate the funding organization to provide each agency a list containing the name, address, and amount pledged for each designating donor.

To foster an impression of enthusiastic support, the PMHA encourages all volunteers and state hospital employees to make designations to the Association; and it rewards their compliance with paid-up membership. Since the agency is technically within its rights, the practice cannot be legitimately prohibited; however, the Fund's annoyance with the imposed clerical task has become the subject of an annual dialogue. Although these interchanges are usually conducted unofficially (i.e., on coffee break) and are carried on in lowered voices, on one occasion the argument took place before a cafeteria line audience. In a confrontation with the Association executive, the Fund representative raised his voice and angrily demanded: "What the hell do you think we're running, a goddam popularity contest?" (Field notes).

Control of Setting

The struggle of agencies to maintain an impression of autonomy can be illustrated by the significance attached to the control of setting in any performance involving Fund and affiliate. *Going up* to the Fund office is regarded as placing oneself in the position of supplicant, while forcing Fund personnel to *come down* to an agency office is perceived as a demonstration that the agency is not subordinate. Thus, saving face requires the devising of ingenious strategems. An executive, caught with no convenient excuse for avoiding a summons upstairs will agree, then have a secretary phone, plead an unanticipated emergency, and invite the Fund representative to a later meeting in the agency office. The Fund employee demurs and reschedules the invitation upstairs. The executive apologizes for a previous engagement, etc., etc. In some cases, the deadlock can be resolved only by a compromise setting in an outside restaurant or the ever neutral arena of the cafeteria.

Cooperative Concealment

Much of the difference in Fund and Affiliate viewpoints stems from the fact that the United Fund deals with the buyer (i.e., the person who pays for the service) and is therefore a sales organization; while the agency, as a supplier of services, is ostensibly oriented to the consumer (i.e., the client). In spite of these different frames of reference, the interdependence of Fund and affiliates makes the concealment of discreditable information mutually advantageous. Thus, when the Fund makes the claim that "only six cents on the dollar are spent on administration, while *94% of your donation goes directly to those in need,"*[4] agencies remain discreetly quiet and cooperatively list salaries as "services." This statement is patently misleading unless, of course, agency staff members qualify as "those in need."

As another example, when the Fund points with pride to the fact that its promotional luncheons are paid for by local businesses and industries and not one cent comes from campaign funds, agency executives content themselves with observing to each other that this is, nonetheless, an expense which is borne by the community, and money which is diverted from the needs of clients.

On the other side of the coin, agencies also distort information in meeting the United Fund requirements for quantifiable public relations data. Annually, a Fund questionnaire to affiliates (for promotion information) asks for "number of people served by agency." Since Mental Health actually serves very few clients[5] it suffers by comparison with status quo agencies. Therefore, people "served" are arbitrarily defined as all the patients in all the mental hospitals, all the people who request booklets, all the volunteers who are provided educational experiences by participating in the work of the Association (including those who contribute to the Christmas campaign), and all the people in all the audiences at Association functions or at meetings addressed by a member of the Speaker's Bureau. The sum total is an impressive public relations figure which becomes a part of a larger total calculated to enhance the collective image.

COOPERATING ORGANIZATION

One of the professed advantages of unified funding is the integration of agencies and the elimination of overlapping services. Hence, although all United Fund Affiliates are engaged in vigorous competition for financial allocations and volunteers, they are simultaneously expected to sustain an impression of an integrated, cooperative work force. For this cooperation to be enthusiastic, there must be mutual benefits for the agencies and fringe benefits for participating staff members.

Ordinarily, public demonstrations of cooperative effort are arranged through programs in which a single agency is the sponsor and a large number of "cooperating organizations" provide supportive effects. To accomplish such a show of unity, each agency involved loans a staff member to serve on an advisory board or steering committee. In such cases, the ubiquitous luncheon becomes a performance in which the audience is composed of colleagues.

Goffman (1959: 159-166) defines colleagues as "persons who present the same routine to the same kind of audience, but who do not participate together as teammates do, at the same time and place before the same particular audience." Thus, when colleagues become an audience, as at a steering committee meeting, they are a wise audience and the performance becomes a show like that which real actors stage at Academy Awards Presentations. The format is very similar to the dramaturgy staged for volunteers except that there is little audience mystification. The ritual of introductions and the inspirational segment of the meeting are merely familiar routines reciprocally endured so that each member of the audience will have his share of recognition.

Cooperation is End Rather Than Means

The motivation for accepting a steering committee assignment may stem from a sincere interest in the project and an honest desire to be helpful. However, cooperation often serves ends other than those intended by the sponsor.

Among the objectives of the participating agency is the acquisition of the label "cooperative" and the prestigious status of serving in an advisory capacity. Additionally, in the same action by which an agency enlarges its own scope of activity, it is also able to protect its territorial boundaries from invasion by the sponsoring group. Thus, although the participation segment of the meeting involves a perfunctory acceptance of most of the host agency's proposals, participants are alert for any suggestion which might be considered detrimental to their vested interests.

For the staff member who becomes the cooperative observer in the competitor's camp, one of the least, but at the same time one of the more attractive advantages is the respite from his own dramaturgical responsibilities. And although he may profess a reluctance to leave his own work, it is common knowledge that the luncheon meeting extending into company time has a much higher attendance than the after hours session. Further, in representing his agency, the cooperator not only increases his professional status, but also has an opportunity to make himself more attractive to other agencies, thereby enhancing his negotiating position in relation to his own career. A long list of committee memberships is evidence for the personnel committee that the employee is becoming a professional mover and shaker. And in the last analysis, it is this which will assure him upward mobility—or at the very least, an impressive obituary.

Limitations and Extensions

Aside from the committee exchanges, the extent of cooperation has definite limitations. With discretion, sentiments concerning the United Fund may be shared; but techniques for increasing allocations may not. Volunteers are shared with reluctance and hostility; but clients tend to be regarded as highly valued ritual objects to be passed from one agency to another through an elaborate system of rites and ceremonies reminiscent of the Kula ring.

Although the Mental Health Association maintains twenty-four hour service in its residential rehabilitation center, the agency observes the schedule restrictions common to all private agencies in regard to the walk-in client who has not been "properly" processed. The cardinal rule which these clients must observe is that problems are to be confined to the 37½ hour work week.

Agency staff members are not officially available for crises occurring after hours or on weekends. And while a volunteer can and does call staff members at home, the client who is so presumptuous is usually referred elsewhere or given an office hours appointment. In the event that a social worker is absent from the office, staff members who are not professional social workers are expected not to become involved with a client beyond minimal courtesy. In a typical incident, a staff member confronted by an exhausted, disturbed, and fundless "walk-in" fifteen minutes before closing time, provided money for a night's lodging from personal funds and was severely criticized. The admonishment: "Such action contributes to dependency. He should have been sent to the Salvation Army." Thus, the unprofessional but dedicated staff member learns that his dedication should be directed to volunteers rather than clients.

The inability to provide emergency help is deplored by both professionals and nonprofessionals. However, the rationally organized United Fund affiliate is expected to observe business hours; and there are no emergency monies which can be disbursed to a "deserving" family at staff discretion.

If, in the Good Samaritan Foundation building, the un-deserving poor are not so much those who are shiftless as those who do not show proper respect for staff schedules, the private agency is not unique in this respect. In fact, the entire referral system is complicated by the universality of the observance of the five day week. Even death is subject to holidays. In a recent incident, a heart attack victim who died on the city streets on a Friday afternoon was taken to the County Hospital morgue. The family, attempting to claim the body, was informed that it could only be released by a deputy sheriff who would not be available before Monday.

Since mental patients tend to have many problems, it is not unusual for one client to be involved either serially or simultaneously with numerous agencies. In one case, an ambulatory schizophrenic whose handicaps were complicated by an overwhelming body odor was passed on with such alacrity that he became a referral record holder.

Ordinarily however, each referral involves such a complexity of paper work, delays, deferred appointments, and re-referrals that the attrition rate of clients lost in transit is very high. At County hospital, for example—which accounts for some 14,000 outside referrals annually—as many as fifty percent of the patients are "lost" even in intrahospital referrals (Field notes).

Families involved with numerous agencies are labeled "multiple agency families" and are considered "hard core problems." Little attention is give the possibility that the hard core problem may be the ritualistic referral system.

For the PMHA, it should be noted that the referral of the walk-in client is consistent with the agency's manifest function. The Association has never professed to be a treatment facility. Even its residential rehabilitation center was designed as a pioneer project to demonstrate the feasibility of a transitional care program.

THE COOPERATION OF MEDIA

In examining the symbiotic relationships between agencies, we find that organizations which could be expected to use countervailing power to exercise social control are frequently immobilized or self-immobilizing. This situation is not unusual among groups mutually engaged in spending public monies; however, it does make society increasingly dependent upon media for exposure of activity which might be considered detrimental to the public interest.

We have previously discussed the means by which all agency expenditures—from flash bulbs to expense account luncheons—come to be defined as "services to the community." But the private social welfare agency also receives cooperation from media to a degree unknown to tax supported welfare organizations.

Some of this support is subtle. Where business is forced to make its claims in *paid advertisements*, agency promotion is defined as *news*. Business buys radio and TV *commercials*; agencies are given time for "*public service announcements*" or "*messages in the public interest.*"

An audience will suffer the exaggerations of the advertiser and discount his claims; but it tends to accept those statements which are presented in the public interest news format—especially when such communications provide justification for the morality of delegated humanitarianism. Thus, an agency can make almost any claim within the realm of credibility with the assurance that the desired information will be communicated. News stories may be condensed and superlatives deleted, but the agency's public relations figures are neither changed nor challenged.

Another type of subtle support is that which precludes the initiation of any investigation which might result in unfavorable publicity for any affiliate in good standing with the United Fund. This courtesy to private agencies (which are supported by what in many cases is coerced philanthropy) is not extended to tax-supported agencies. Moreover, although the United Fund and its affiliates are unquestioningly supported, the client remains fair game; and the mental patient continues to be branded as a potential menace.

The cooperation of media is not purely altruistic. Richard Carter (1961: 266) notes that in all cases, United Funds have been begotten by business and industry whose interest lies in eliminating in-plant solicitation and broadening the base of philanthropy. The communication industries are themselves largescale employers and thus share this interest. But beyond that, they are also dependent upon the large economic organizations for advertising revenue.

There is, then, no countervailing power to keep the PMHA on target. The State Association, dependent upon the Pangloss chapter for funds, has a vested interest in the organization's success in mobilizing resources. The Fund and its affiliates cooperate in concealing discreditable information for the sake of the collective image. And media helps sustain the favorable definition in the interests of convenience.

Thus, unless the object of the action can make himself heard, there is nothing to prevent the substitution of image manipulation for goal-directed action. The demands of the environment are filled by the dramatization of virtue. And the association which fulfills these demands is rewarded.

10
THE IMAGERY OF
CHRISTMAS

The relationship between the Mental Health Association and the state mental hospital system is one which the new agency employee finds perplexing. On one occasion, the Association is protector and defender: while on another, it is a severe critic and viewer-with-alarm. In one circumstance, it is deferential: in another, it is aggressive and arrogant. For every situation there appears to be a different definition and a different approach.

The ambiguity in the situation is directly related to the fact that the agency vacilates between being *against mental illness* and being *for mental health*. To crusade in behalf of the patient requires an aggresive campaign against hospital deficiencies. To emphasize prevention requires that people be encouraged to seek early treatment. Since anxiety can intensify emotional disturbance, and since exposure of detrimental hospital conditions increases the anxiety of potential patients and their families, the Association attempts to avoid self-defeating tactics by playing pivot position. In "speaking for those who cannot speak for themselves," it cannot condone hospital conditions; on the other hand, in speaking to legislators in behalf of better hospital pay schedules, it cannot devalue the people whom it is championing. By and large, since legislative activities take place during only a few months of the year, the Association takes a "hard line" in its relations with the hospitals.

The ambivalence of the Association evokes from hospital personnel an attitude of grudging cooperation. Except for legislative activities, official PMHA Hospital Volunteer Programs are skillfully deflected or politely frustrated everywhere except at the Sunnyview State Hospital. Although this particular hospital urgently needs help and the agency needs an outlet for volunteers, there are many problems. Foremost is the sensitivity of the hospital staff to criticism. What the Association staff calls "interpreting the needs of the hospital" is considered by the hospital staff to be the foregone conclusion that "Sunnyview is always wrong."

An avowal of public apathy in worn red brick, Sunnyview State Hospital is an overcrowded, understaffed facility with some 2,000 patients of whom more than half (females) are housed in a four story relic of Victorian architecture. Bedrooms without electricity, turn-of-the-century plumbing, clutter, cockroaches, rats and garbage are outstanding characteristics of its depressing environment. Some years ago, after repeated warnings that the nearly hundred-year-old building was a firetrap, legislators pondered the problem and in due time arrived at a solution: an arrangement was made for the construction of a fire station on hospital grounds.

This, however, was real progress in comparison with the 1857 legislature. At that time, by failing to make any appropriation at all, the lawmakers forced the hospital to close its doors and "return upon the counties the miserable beings who were undergoing treatment there" (Williams, 1950: 80).

Optimism is foreign to Sunnyview. For many patients, it is limbo. One third of the inmates are over sixty, and many of the others have exhausted all other possibilities of treatment. It is the state's oldest hospital and it operates on the state's lowest perdiem cost per patient.

In spite of the hopelessness which pervades this institution, there are staff members and administrators whose efforts are quietly heroic. They voluntarily accept working conditions which are no less miserable than patients' living conditions. They share the same roaches, stenches, heat and dreary over-crowded environs.

There are other employees, who, like the patients, are social rejects. In its urban location and with its meager budget, the hospital cannot compete in a tight labor market. According to a hospital informant, in a recent class of forty male attendant trainees, two were victims of extracurricular homicides, twenty-eight dropped out for less compelling reasons, and the ten who were certified used their diplomas to obtain better-paid employment in nursing homes.

Of Association criticism, a staff member said:

> They [the Association] simply cannot realize that sometimes we are lucky to have one attendant covering three wards. Believe me, under those conditions, you just can't run the place like Menninger's [Field notes].

The hospital's need for volunteers and the Association's eagerness to provide are not completely compatible. In any hospital, but especially in a psychiatric facility, an untrained, unsupervised volunteer can be a menace. And at Sunnyview, the staff shortage is so acute that training and supervision are very difficult. In addition, although the Association professes that its Mental Health Hospital Volunteers are the only "official" volunteers, the hospital staff must cope with sixty other volunteer groups who come in at more or less regular intervals.

As was previously mentioned, the Association's bias for the patient is perceived by the hospital staff as anti-hospital. A hospital employee said:

Volunteers will believe anything a patient tells them, and the Association believes the volunteers. We had one patient—a magpie—who had accumulated 20 slips, 11 winter coats, and three shoe boxes full of matched sets of jewelry, along with an assortment of food—and most of it was hidden under the floorboards in her room. Meantime, relatives were screaming because clothing belonging to other patients had disappeared. We discovered her cache because her room was swarming with cockroaches—and of course, we had to clean it out completely. The patient complained to a volunteer that the nurse had taken away all her things. The Association fired off a letter to the Division accusing us of "redistributing a patient's private possessions." Wouldn't you think they'd at least have had the courtesy to check with us first? [Field notes].

If the Association acted, in this instance, with undue haste, there is evidence that the hospital and the Association are capable of extensive cooperation in concealing destructive information. The best example of such efforts is the Christmas program.

OPERATION SNOWBALL

Operation Snowball is the Association's most ambitious program. It involves the collection, inspection, gift wrapping, and distribution of Christmas presents to patients in all Pangloss County public psychiatric wards. The project requires hundreds of volunteers, almost one third of the year's total staff time, miles of ribbon and wrapping paper, and thousands of dollars' worth of contributed gifts.

Planning for the event begins in earnest in July or August with the appointment of a General Chairman whose commitment will require from 300 to 500 volunteer hours. In late November, collection depots are opened all over the city, and early December is the beginning of a ten to fifteen day gift wrapping marathon with volunteers from many civic organizations assembled at a designated headquarters. The climax of the project is an individual party for every ward at Sunnyview and County hospitals, and a combined-ward party at University Hospital.

Operation Snowball is an excellent example of a program which has become a hallowed and sacred tradition. Several hundred philanthropic groups make it their traditional Christmas charity, and it is universally supported by churches in the community. The Executive, staff, and some Board members privately express the view that the program has become a millstone, but they fear that its abandonment would be equated with the Association's abandonment of mental patients.

There is also the matter of public relations. In a typical year, Operation Snowball will be the subject of more than half the agency's total newspaper publicity, a concentrated barrage of radio and television spot announcements worth several hundred thousand dollars, plus sentimental seasonal tie-ins on newsbroadcasts and interview programs.

The program originated in the midwest and has spread across the country. A former Executive Director of a California Mental Health Association made this evaluation:

> The program is a fantastic gimmick. I doubt that it does the patient much good, but the publicity is tremendous. Worthwhile too. Even if we took all the gifts and dumped them in the Bay, anytime you can get somebody to go out and buy a present for a patient, that person is becoming aware of the patients' needs [Field notes].

CLIENTS COME LAST

The point is controversial. Some staff members, as well as a minority of the Board, believe that the program provides a kind of "cheap grace"—i.e., an easy means by which an individual can reduce his guilt feelings. They argue that Operation Snowball is a device which provides the opportunity for people to substitute a short term investment for a long range tax commitment, and thus it functions to preserve the status quo. And finally, there is the belief that the program was once valid, but that now, with greater public awareness, it serves only to reinforce the notion that mental patients are rejects.

As in most public relations efforts, the Christmas project involves both the publicity and performance techniques of image manipulation. The publicity creates an image, and the mobilization of activity is designed to sustain the fostered impression.

Of all agency programs, the Christmas project encompasses the greatest concealment of destructive information. To clarify the discrepancies requires a point by point analysis of the larger issues.

Fostered Impression: Need

In news releases, the Association's definition of the situation is that hospitalized mental patients are miserable, sad, lonely, and forgotten at Christmas time. Their only means of knowing that "someone in the community cares" is through the presents and parties provided by the Mental Health Association.

DESTRUCTIVE INFORMATION:

Granted that hospitalized patients are miserable, sad, and lonely, they are not forgotten at Christmas. In addition to the elaborate hospital-sponsored party (with gifts) on Christmas, a Sunnyview staff member reported:

> We are absolutely deluged by community organizations giving Christmas parties. Our big꞉ st problem is scheduling. Some wards have as many as fifteen. Of course, they are not all of the same caliber, and they don't all have entertainment—so the patients become downright discriminating [Field notes].

Fostered Impression: Gratitude

The fostered impression that gifts are gratefully received, that the patients "know you care," and that this makes their Christmas happy, is designed to increase the empathic involvement and satisfaction of the donor. The occasional, but extremely rare, thank you note from a patient is quoted and exhibited.

DESTRUCTIVE INFORMATION:

Many patients are not even aware of the nature of the gift, let alone its source. At one Association party, a pathetic old man who received after-shave powder in a metal flask type container nearly choked when he attempted to drink it. Patients who are aware are frequently dissatisfied and do not hesitate to complain. According to a Sunnyview staff member:

> Last year, for instance, there was one attendant—she fights for her patients like a mother hen came down to the office, put her hands on her hips and said, "Miz K., can't you please find me some nice rich Episcopalians for my ward. We're so damn tired of those poor Baptists—all they ever bring is cookies" [Field notes].

In the outside world, and especially in the gift buying middle class, failure to be properly grateful is often considered a symptom of incipient moral turpitude. The ritual of gift giving demands a reciprocal ritual of gratitude. Further, gifts are objects to be treated with respect.

The lack of public understanding of mental illness makes patients' attitudes toward gifts destructive information. In the hospital, it is not at all unusual for the patient to discard the gift and carefully preserve the wrapping paper. Gifts are further profaned by becoming objects of barter. In the swapping process, which often begins while the party is still in progress, an expensive gift may be cheerfully traded for a pack of cigarets. On wards where gifts are apt to be conspicuously profaned, parties are given by hospital volunteers with ward experience, rather than by community philanthropic organizations. Thus, the fiction of the patient's gratitude is preserved.

There are other cases of ingratitude which cannot be considered symptomatic. Sometimes the patient who appears withdrawn and uncommunicative at the official party is *actually* sad, lonely, and miserable because his weekend leave was cancelled. To facilitate the complicated bookkeeping of Operation Snowball, all movement (transfers) of patients between wards is halted at the beginning of the gift wrapping operation. To avoid disappointment of volunteer party givers, patients eligible for a weekend pass are kept in the wards the day of the party. Thus, the hospital's cooperation with the Association is oriented to volunteer satisfaction rather than patients' welfare.

Fostered Impression: 10,000 Gifts

To enhance the project by magnifying its size, Association publicity claims that 10,000 gifts are necessary. To spur donations and to foster the impression that an accurate inventory is being kept, periodic bulletins are issued to the press to the effect that a *specific* number of gifts are still required.

DESTRUCTIVE INFORMATION:

There has never been anything approaching an accurate count, and 10,000 is a public relations figure—i.e., a mythical number. There are actually about 2,500 patients, each patient gets both a large and small gift, which brings the total required to 5,000. Since gifts range from a box of Kleenex (beautifully wrapped) to a $15 smoking jacket, it is often necessary to combine several donations to make one gift. Although the number of gifts needed at any given time are estimates, exact figures—e.g., 3,817—are used to give naive statisticians the impression of accurate inventories. During the last week, the "panic button press releases" are standard procedure in which an engineered emergency provides a means of securing extra publicity and extracting the maximum number of donations from the procrastinators, the ambivalent, and those who might be persuaded to give again. The over-the-top release is the last: it announces that once again the Association has successfully reached its goal.

Fostered Impression: Shared Joy

The impression that working at the gift wrapping center provides a heartwarming experience with the generosity of the community is carefully fostered as a means of getting volunteers.

DESTRUCTIVE INFORMATION:

The wrapping center does provide some amazing examples of generosity; however, on many occasions wrappers complain that gifts are inappropriate. There have also been instances when inspectors have discovered that some of the most elegantly wrapped packages (often those which have been collected at club meetings) indicate that not all the mentally disturbed are hospitalized. In addition to discards, packages have included a box of jagged pieces of broken glass, a file, a soiled corset, condoms, false teeth, and gold rimmed spectacles.

Fostered Impression: Personalized Evidence of Your Concern

The impression is given that each patient receives a personalized gift, chosen from a list of his desires which is provided by ward attendants.

DESTRUCTIVE INFORMATION:

The first ward barrels are filled with careful attention to lists; however, by the last few days, lists are abandoned and patients get whatever is available. That patients keep the gifts for long is doubtful. It is not at all unusual for a ward list to indicate that every patient wears a size 15 shirt and a size 11 sock. Whether this indicates greed, or merely sloth, on the part of the list maker, the patient's Christmas cheer is bound to be diminished. Gifts that are not displaced in the hospital laundry are usually swapped, stolen, or given away. Mental hospitals provide few opportunities for the protection of personal property.

Collusion

The tenth annual Christmas campaign was much like any other except for two details: the chairman was an unusually imaginative and energetic volunteer, and, for the first time, the Association employed a publicist for the project promotion. Previously, the campaign had been called "Operation Santa Claus." On the grounds that this title was demeaning to patients, and also that it did not lend itself to headlines, a new name was adopted. This novelty, plus the outstanding volunteer leadership, resulted in extraordinary press coverage. However, before the project reached its successful climax, it became obvious there was a strong undercurrent of hostility between the chief volunteers and the hospital staff.

At the campaign's end, the General Chairman submitted a detailed report urgently recommending an immediate meeting between volunteers, hospital, and Association representatives so that problems could be discussed and the program evaluated in terms of "better future planning." She further suggested that the Association conduct future wrapping operations at a location other than the hospital's Old Infirmary building; and that it demand that security measures be instituted at the hospital for the protection of patients' property.

When pressed for reasons for the recommended changes, she accused hospital employees of theft. She alleged that Christmas gifts had been stolen from the wrapping room prior to the parties; and that one ward had been systematically stripped of gifts immediately after its party.

In investigating, the Association Volunteer Director discovered that although there was no corroborating evidence to support the first charge, the second could be substantiated.

There had been witnesses to the theft of gifts from a ward. Hospital employees had been seen loading party booty into a hospital truck while patients were in the dining hall.

Aware that the information was potentially damaging, the staff member presented her findings to the Executive Director and advice was sought from the State Association office.

The situation was explosive. The volunteer, indignant at what she considered to be a "betrayal of public trust," was also the close friend and neighbor of an editor whose help had contributed much to the success of the gift drive. An expose was a real possibility.

The discussion of the problem centered around two alternatives: to expose or to conceal. Either action was considered hazardous. As the professed protector of the patient, the Association had a moral obligation to demand an investigation by both the hospital and the governmental unit responsible for hospitals. It was recognized that if this investigation were demanded by the newspaper, rather than the Association, there would be no possibility of controlling destructive information. Moreover, knowledge of the Association's failure to initiate action would be inconsistent with the fostered image of crusader.

On the other hand, there were strong arguments against exposure. If the theft were revealed, confidence in the Christmas program would be destroyed. Further, since the general public tends to have little understanding of the differentiation between public and private agencies, a scandal relevant to the hospital would also be detrimental to the Association.

To further complicate matters, the Association was faced with the imminent convening of the legislature. Inasmuch as one of the most crucial proposals of its legislative program was increased pay for hospital employees, there was great reluctance to jeopardize the bill by the exposure of information which would almost assuredly put legislators and the public in a punitive mood.

The dilemma was finally resolved by the decision to do nothing. The Association would gamble on the editor's discretion. The staff member was assigned the task of cooling out the volunteer. She accepted the assignment, but insisted that there be a private confrontation with the hospital administrator, and that the volunteer's suggestions on the wrapping center and security measures be implemented.

The confrontation did not take place until the following October, and was little more than a formality. The agency executive director called attention to "certain irregularities which must be corrected," and the hospital administrator replied these irregularities had been investigated, and that although no conclusive evidence had been found, employees had been informed that, henceforth, stealing would not be tolerated.

In following the volunteer's recommendations for changes, the Volunteer Director learned that simple solutions applied to complex problems can produce unforeseen results. By moving the gift wrapping operation out into the community, the cooperation of attendants in filling ward barrels with appropriate gifts necessitated long absences from the wards and intensified the hospital's acute shortage of help. Moreover, the hospital staff's cooperation in instituting security procedures was described by Christmas Volunteers as "simply awful." One of them protested:

It was degrading to patients and it completely ruined our party. They made each one take his gift to a table and open it in the presence of two attendants who wrote down its description and the patient's name. When the line got too long, they'd keep telling the patients to "hurry it up"—and if the patient was too slow, they'd rip off the wrappings for him. Some Christmas! [Field notes].

Growth of Empathy

In the beginning, the true believer from the Mental Health Association shares the official point of view that "the patient is always right." However, the seasoned staff member who works closely with hospital staff experiences a subversive counter-socialization.

The hospital staff's accusation that "the Association is primarily interested in publicizing the Association" is sometimes very difficult to refute.

11
THE ALIENATION OF STAFF

In the studies of voluntary association, many observers have focused on the disaffection and alienation of the volunteer. But the bureaucratization of voluntarism has alienating effects which are not limited to the unpaid workers. For staff members as well, role requirements can be the source of progressive disenchantment.

The initial change from idealist to pragmatist, from sincere recruit to dedicated cynic, is accomplished by self-deception. However, staff experiences make self-deception difficult to maintain. Disillusionment is a cumulative process.

Staff Characteristics

In the seven year period covered by this study, seven individuals attempted to fill the roles of the Volunteer Director and Education Director. Two of these persons found themselves misfits within the first month of employment and did not complete the training period.[1] The other five stayed with the Association for periods ranging from seventeen to sixty-two months. Their age range was from thirty to fifty-two years. The mean years of education completed was fifteen.

Although each of the five possessed unique talents, common characteristics made their role performances very much alike. All were enthusiastic and energetic in their implementation of existing programs, and all were creative and innovative in devising projects and attempting to find new approaches to old problems. Each had experienced early socialization in the tradition of the Protestant ethic, and each was deeply committed to the social reform aspects of the role.

All resigned.

Severance Pattern

For the Associate Directors who remained with the Association for more than three months, the pattern of severance was without much variation. Each discovered that charm, cajolery, and temperament were ineffective means of persuasion for producing desired change. *Each resigned formally at least twice*, and all confessed to having *threatened to resign more times than they could remember*. None left the agency because of a better offer; none left because of salary dissatisfaction. Four have since experienced sharp upward mobility in their careers; and the fifth has retired.

Those who are now working have continued in mental health or a related discipline. Two are involved with mental health programs or planning at the state level. The remaining two resumed education in behavioral sciences. No one has gone into "legitimate business."

Role Suicide

The history of threat, attempt, and finally successful destruction of the role self follows a behavioral pattern not unlike that of the suicide. When the threat—the "Cry for Help" (Farberow and Schniedman, 1961)— is ignored and the individual does not succeed in effecting change in the situational details which he feels are unbearable, he tends to progress to more drastic measures. The final act by which he removes himself from the offending environment and eliminates the offensive role is punishing to both self and others. As an act of aggression, role suicide is the ultimate protest. The typical fantasy is "You'll be sorry when I'm gone" (Stengel, 1964: 45).

Examination of the pre- and post-severance behavior of Associate Directors indicates that their principal reason for resignation was the failure of the organizational structure to provide gratification for personal needs. Primarily this failure was in the areas of self-determination, self-expression, expression of values, and self-identification (Katz and Kahn, 1966: 336-347).

Self-Determination

In each resignation, the point of crucial conflict was executive interference. "Refusal to delegate," "overoccupation with detail," "no respect for my intelligence," and "mixing in" were some of the phrases used to describe the situation. Staff members commented:

> The executive is basically a nice guy. But he doesn't trust anyone else to make a decision. He never showed any confidence in my ability or intelligence—even after several years [Field notes].

> I kept promising myself I wouldn't get emotionally involved. But when he started in on details I wanted to scream.... Having to justify and explain every action was insulting and a waste of time. Other people have considered me fairly competent [Field notes].

The many complaints in this area were very much the same, and all were relevant to staff status and to the directive dominance exercised by the Executive. However, the Executive's close supervision of the details of every routine produced a finished performance which was dramaturgically professional. His anticipation of potential performance disruptions required that alternate plans be provided for every possible contingency and that everyone be fully informed in advance in regard to those plans. A staff member gave an example:

> We had planned an all-day program at Sunnyview for prospective teenage volunteers. We hoped for 200 reservations and got 700. I had been in continuous communication with hospital personnel—they were really nervous—and although it was a complex program, I felt I had everything nailed down. At the last minute, the executive decided we needed a mimeographed time schedule just so we'd look organized. We already had printed programs and I was annoyed—as a protest, I made up a time table in what I thought was ridiculously exaggerated detail with split second timing for everything. But the silly thing worked! The Sunnyview people followed that schedule as if their lives depended on it. It was a case where looking good produced good results [Field notes].

The problem with the perfectionist approach is that while it minimizes performance disruptions, it contributes to tension and greatly increases the work load of staff. In addition, although this sort of detail was over-communicated, important policy information was withheld. In either case, the action increased status anxiety.

Self-Expression

The gratification an individual derives from expressing his talents and abilities is heightened when those talents and abilities are recognized by others. In Mental Health, the public performance requires of staff not only self-abnegation, but also the presentation of a demeaned self. For an individual who has been labeled "professional" to be nothing more than the custodian of the idiot sheet, carrier of chairs, and adjustor of p.a. system is to play a discrepant role. When the staff person successfully fosters the impression that no impression is being fostered, when the volunteer is sincerely convinced that he alone has done the work and he alone deserves the praise, the staff member relegates himself to the role of non-person (Goffman, 1959: 141-166). And the greater this role success, the greater is the amount of feedback depreciating the self-image.

The resentment which accompanies the depreciation of self is a source of guilt and a sentiment which cannot be freely shared. The true-believing idealist commits himself selflessly. He therefore perceives his desire for recognition as selfish and unworthy.

Another source of expressive satisfaction is the successful completion of a project. Role overload made this kind of gratification rare. Staff members said:

> When I finally quit, I was handling so many projects that I wasn't doing anything well. It wasn't the work I minded. It was always feeling guilty and apologetic [Field notes].

> We never finished or really evaluated anything. I think we did much that was worthwhile, but we never really knew. After a while you had so many doubts that everything seemed trivial [Field notes].

Expression of Values

Very much akin to self expression (expression of abilities and talents) is the expression, both verbal and nonverbal, of one's moral viewpoint. Although being an employee of the Mental Health Association provided the means of demonstrating a career choice of service to others, role requirements often made the expression of beliefs and values indiscreet, if not impossible. Value orientations common to all of the staff members included egalitarianism (at least within one's own social stratum), humanitarianism, sincerity, and democratic process.

EGALITARIANISM:

As a social agency improves its image, it tends to attract a "better class" of volunteers. Top agencies—i.e., United Fund and Metropolitan Services Council—are distinguished by board representation from the upper class and the Establishment. While Mental Health has not reached this level, during the course of this study it moved from predominately middle to upwardly mobile upper-middle-class participation, and for special projects has recruited from the "lively arts crowd" who constitute the Pangloss version of the elite. Themselves members of the lower echelons of the upper middle class, Associate Directors experienced difficulty in mustering the expected amount of deference to people they considered peers. An attitude common to all was expressed as follows:

> I found bowing and scraping to be downright degrading. I also felt the demands for gratitude were excessive. There's some-thing about volunteering that brings out the cat in women and the cad in men. Some of the men treated you like a servant.

But the women emphasized their superiority with remarks like "My dear, I'd love to have an interesting job like yours, but *my* husband won't let me work." I always felt like telling them that *my* husband doesn't have such a shaky ego [Field notes].

Many of our volunteers were simply great, but one witch per program is enough to take the joy out of the job. And unfortunately, they're such unforgettable witches [Field notes].

HUMANITARIANISM:

This was a value which staff members expected volunteers to share. When they did not, it was a source of disillusionment. One staff member observed:

The only way I can keep my faith in humanity is to avoid getting to know volunteers socially. An experience that was especially awful was at a party with a group of my favorite hospital volunteers—people you would expect to be compassionate. They spent the entire evening damning everybody on welfare. And nobody flinched when one of them said: "What makes me boil is spending all that money for the Blind School. Landscaping and beautiful buildings for kids that can't even see!" [Field notes].

SINCERITY:

The moral terms on which staff members judge the world may be ironic in view of the fact that they themselves are accomplished manipulators. Nevertheless, they admire sincerity and find it a virtue which is in short supply. One of them commented:

I hate working on benefits. We did this one for mentally ill children—to me this is one of the most heartbreaking tragedies a family can experience. At any rate, when we took the Mental Health posters to the committee, they protested violently. The chairman said, "We don't want those depressing things! This is supposed to be a fun affair." I really didn't expect them to cry all evening—but surely they could have stood the pain of knowing what they were spending their money for [Field notes].

A staff member who was exceptionally successful in maintaining the ingratiating front was asked if she ever felt hypocritical. In relation to her own sincerity, she replied:

You just have to be a ham—pure ham—don't you see. And I never let up. I've gotten so used to hamming it up that I almost never go out of character [Field notes].

DEMOCRATIC PROCESS:

While all staff members pay lip service to this value, the degree of commitment varies. One employee, a former patient who strenuously resisted the transition from sincere recruit to dedicated cynic, was a conscientious worker with a higher degree of commitment to the patient than to the agency. A devout Episcopalian, she began to be disenchanted with the Association during the time of the initial expansion of the public relations program. Prior to her resignation, she protested the changing policy to the Board President and confronted the Executive and her co-worker with the accusation.

All that you care about is efficiency and publicity. I will not use your 'completed staff plan.' It's nothing more than a device for manipulating volunteers and it's an insult to their intelligence. The whole business violates every principle of democratic process [Field notes].

A different opinion was:

Committee meetings are a Godawful waste. If you don't have a completed staff plan you get bogged down in endless discussions of trivia. Why shouldn't I be the one to define the problem and specify the objectives? This is my area of competence. They don't have to buy it [Field notes].

Personality Conflict?

In a situation characterized by interpersonal conflict there is always the possibility that the problem may be rooted in abrasive personalities and/or conflict of values. However, since the complaints of staff are common to many agencies, it is probable that the selection of a certain type personality for the superordinate position is determined by the role itself; and that the values by which the agency is guided and regulated are specified by the requirements of the Executive's performance.

Although staff members were critical of the PMHA Executive, every criticism was tempered with admiration and a certain amount of self blame. Every staff member expressed the opinion that the Executive had a deep concern for the mentally ill, a willingness to admit mistakes, and an ability to land on his feet. He was described as a person who "could turn a disaster into an advantage." The underlying attitude—"He is successful, therefore he must be right"—reflects an unconscious acknowledgement of the dominant American value.

The Executive Role

   Like the staff, the Executive also performed discrepant roles. His policy of "no personal publicity" was deplored by the staff:

> Other agency executives are sometimes quoted, have their pictures in the papers, and have some prestige in the community. In Mental Health, nobody even knows who the executive is. He's the out-of-breath character carrying in the extra chairs [Field notes].

   Here again is an instance where there are reciprocal consequences relevant to personal fronts. When the highest ranking staff member is a non-person, all ranks are deflated. Whether the Board members expected this degree of self-effacement is not as important as the fact that the Executive perceived such an expectation as consistent with his role. And the Board accepted his interpretation.

Self-Identification

   For an individual to internalize an organization's goals, it is necessary that the requirements of him, as an instrument of implementation, are appropriate to his self-concept. The volunteer accepts roles with no monetary reward because society regards such roles as having intrinsic value, and because his behavior is reinforced by other volunteers with high status with whom he can identify.

   The staff person, on the other hand, by accepting payment for a role which requires self-abnegation, experiences self-alienation. The demands of appropriate deference and demeanor prohibit him from expressing his own values, and identification with fellow staff members who are also non-persons provides diminishing satisfaction.

Belief that the means—the performance routines—justify the end is further undermined when the performer begins to identify with the audience rather than his teammates. As the agency Volunteer Director comes to understand the problems of the Hospital Volunteer Director, bonds of empathy are established. Interaction between the two is frequent, sentiments of liking increase, and maintaining the professed opposition between agency and hospital becomes increasingly difficult. The realignment creates a situation in which the two directors become teammates in defensive performances directed to volunteers, to the Association, and to the hospital. The agency staff member's realization that much of the agency "help" creates actual hardship for the hospital is conducive to ambivalence and distrust concerning the efficacy of the Association's means in relation to the professed goals.

In the same manner, continuing interaction with "good" volunteers—i.e., working volunteers—creates sentiments of friendship which make manipulative devices increasingly distasteful. The staff person becomes protective and avoids asking such a volunteer to participate in performances requiring the concealment of discreditable information. For example, the Christmas chairmanship is sometimes given to a prima donna. Since staff regards the role requirements as exploitative, and since the prima donna is usually perceived as someone who exploits staff, her selection is justified because she is "deserving." But such a choice does not make staff work easier.

The identification of performer with audience is a process which takes time and is segmental. Good volunteers increase indentification; exploitative volunteers exert a counter force. Thus, a staff members wavers between two loyalties and finds no satisfactory answer to the question: Who am I?

Although a staff member thus caught experiences self-alienation, he continues to have faith in the ultimate attainment of the goal and to hold the belief that the movement is charged with a sacred mission. Since it is the morality of the means which he questions, the threats of resignation are a sanction conditionally imposed in the hope that the worth of self will be affirmed through the institution of the desired situational change—thus reducing the discrepancy between the role self and the idealized self. However, as the employee who insisted on changes in the Christmas program learned, there is no easy solution. Once established, the performance routines define the roles of the performers. Or, as Goffman (1959: 252) maintains, "the self is a *product* of the scene that comes off and not a cause of it."

PSEUDO GEMEINSCHAFT

It is interesting to note that at the time of the successful resignation, each role incumbent blamed the Executive for the impasse—but *several months later, each tended to shift the blame to the Board of Directors*. This was expressed by all of the exemployees in much the same way. Each tended to preface an expression of bitterness with the over-protest: "It isn't that I am bitter about this, but . . ." For each, *loss of faith* in the ultimate attainment of the goal was directly related to *loss of face*. The staff actor's final performance—the sacrifice of the role self—was enacted before an apathetic audience. Here again is the suicide fantasy:

> Suicide is often a means of forcing others to express their love
> even after one's death. Tom Sawyer's success in making a

whole community profess their love for him and their feeling of guilt for not having shown it while he was alive, is a brilliant description of this kind of fantasy come true [Stengel, 1964: 45].

Like Tom Sawyer, the person who executes a role self may attend the last rites and observe the mourners. For the Mental Health performers, the real alienation occurred when their passing was practically unnoticed.

> Oh sure, to my face they carried on about my leaving. Even the president fussed. But did any of them let out a peep at the Board meeting? Of course not! [Field notes].

> It wasn't that I wanted to stay. The situation was irreversible. But we have too many people on our Board who don't know and don't want the others to know what they don't know. The ones who do know couldn't care less about staff members [Field notes].

> It's really kind of ironic, isn't it. Both of us left because we hated manipulating people. But I know now that we were far more *manipulated* than *manipulative* [Field notes].
> The Association uses people. Staff it uses up! [Field notes].

The disillusionment which staff members experienced is again a part of the fabric of self-deception. In protecting "good" Board members, they assumed that admiration and respect were sentiments mutually felt. But the expectation that volunteers would be reciprocally protective was unrealistic in relation to the performance. By writing himself out of the script—by accepting the role of non-person—the staff member made himself expendable.

THE ULTIMATE OUTCOME

At the time of this writing the Pangloss Mental Health Association has no professional staff in community organization positions. The role of Education Director has been unfilled for nearly two years;[2] the Volunteer Director post has been vacant for seven months—in spite of continuous interviewing and advertising.

The situation would seem to indicate one of two possibilities: either the Association is not effectively carrying on its programs, or—the Association has been overstaffed. However, by hiring free-lance publicity writers, the Association has continued to be publicized. And the fact that "important" programs have no staff leadership has largely gone unnoticed.

A second interesting development is that although there is no professional volunteer or education staff, *the Association has doubled its staff of Social Workers.* With the enthusiastic support of the United Fund (a large increase in allocation) plus grants from two Pangloss philanthropic foundations, the PMHA has established a second rehabilitation center for patients making the transition from hospital to community.

Thus, Beers' dream of a dynamic social movement has spawned yet another status quo organization. In becoming an extension of the mental hospital system, the Association moves from "warmer" to "cooler."

12

THE TRAP

In relation to organizational goals, image manipulation has both functional and dysfunctional aspects.

By concealing the reality of volunteer apathy, it creates role discrepancies of such magnitude that alienated staff members stage dramatic (but destructive) protests, and the Executive opts for the safer programs of supportive services.

By operationalizing the norm of most-least, it frustrates the action of the volunteer who has genuine concern.

By protecting the community from factual information about the patient and his circumstances, it increases social distance and preserves the status quo.

By permitting the Association to cling to a program with a high publicity potential but little intrinsic value, it provides society an opportunity to pay off a large obligation with tokenism.

And by becoming an integration mechanism primarily for people who may already be overintegrated, it increases the concentration of power among those who are already powerful.

But it does mobilize resources! It has enabled the Association to foster an image of a vigorous, effective organization; to transcend stigma; to have consistently excellent attendance at meetings; and to increase support from the United Fund.

The question is: *What are they waiting for?* Having mobilized resources, *why does the agency not utilize these resources to escalate action toward its professed goals?* Why must the

Governor of the State establish a Mental Health Planning Commission (1963) to implement action for mental health: *"to set in motion at the grass roots level a movement* which will result in state wide plans for establishing services for the mentally ill and mentally retarded . . ." (Central Region Committee, 1965: 1). Why had the Association not mobilized its own resources in this area?

To find the answers, we must return to the performance. In our previous discussion of relationships of organizations within the associational network, we have shown that when an audience possesses destructive information, it will maintain a cooperative silence if there is a symbiotic relationship between audience and performer which makes such tact mutually advantageous. Moreover, we have indicated that this cooperation is not entirely voluntary, but is rather based on the functional interdependences which enable organizations to survive. The fostered impression of mutual helpfulness is an accommodative process. But if at any time, the professed definition becomes threatening to such an audience, a performance disruption can occur. It may take the form of an open challenge, or it may be handled by a request for a backstage conference—but in either event, it forces a redefinition.

However, in performances staged before voluntary audiences, it is exceedingly rare for the professed reality to be challenged. This is not to say that the routine is flawless. In fact, in spite of the great pains taken to sustain a favorable definition, the dramaturgical devices used by the agency are seldom foolproof in the hands of a volunteer teammate. Performance disruptions do occur: A chairman confronted with an unanticipated contingency becomes flustered and looks helplessly to staff for instruction.. . . A Board President (demonstrating that he is wise to the manipulations of the backstage crew) waves his sheaf of instructions, winks at the audience, and announces, "I've got to look at the idiot sheet to see what to do next".... A shill misses his cue and must be reminded that he has something important to say.... A master of ceremonies, too long at the bar, spices his introductions with risque jokes.... Or, a staff member with mixed loyalties subverts the performance in protecting a volunteer.... And many times, the "most important program ever brought to the community" is merely one more mediocre routine.

But the performance continues. Everyone pretends that nothing is amiss. The working consensus between the actors and the audience is undisturbed. The fostered impression remains unchallenged. The question again is—Why?

Goffman (1959: 232) suggests that

> Audiences are motivated to act tactfully because of an immediate identification with the performers, or because of a desire to avoid a scene, or to ingratiate themselves with the performers for the purposes of exploitation.

Identification and scene avoidance are based on internalized values. The volunteer, as a hero of a democratic participation, is given dramatic dominance because the identifying audience will be predictably respectful. Likewise, recruitment efforts are directed to middle and upper class volunteers because "they understand social organization"—which is to say, they have internalized the middle class norm of scene avoidance. Their reference group is the establishment, and they have been socialized to exhibit public solidarity and to avoid the open exercise of power which can "embarrass their lessers" (Goffman, 1955).

But ingratiation is quite another matter. E. E. Jones (1964: 1-11), who has contributed some very important insights into this social process, defines ingratiation as "a class of strategic behaviors *illicitly designed* to influence a particular other person concerning the attractiveness of one's personal qualities." He suggest that the illicit aspect of the behavior lies in the fact that it is a violation of the normative expectation of honest self-presentation. The ingratiator has an ulterior motive: he attempts to increase his personal attractiveness for the purpose of future benefits.

Heretofore described as a manipulative strategy used by staff to exploit the volunteer, it should be recognized that ingratiation is by no means a one way process. When used by a volunteer, it takes many forms. It may be the pseudo-Gemeinschaft warmth by which a volunteer "cons" a staff member into fulfilling the volunteer's commitment. Or it may be an invitation to a social event in an attempt to obligate a staff member to provide the volunteer a shortcut to performance prominence. It is even the lovely letter with fulsome praise—"you help to strengthen us, sustain us, inspire us . . ." written by the Personnel Committee in belated appreciation of a staff member's decision to refuse a better offer and thus continue to sustain the impression that the Association management inspires sacrificial loyalty.

However, the form of ingratiation which is much more difficult to recognize is that which permits and applauds the collective fabrication of illusions. In such instances, ingratiation is a cooperative undertaking in a public performance where the activity of the team of actors is designed to enhance organizational attractiveness for the sake of organizational gain. The success of the behavior is determined by the gullibility of the target (the audience) or by the target person's willingness to cooperate with other target persons in supporting the misrepresentation for his own ulterior purposes.

THE DEMAND FOR ILLUSIONS

Although ingratiation is often not included among listings of major social processes, it is my contention that as both a process and a motivating force, *ingratiation is the significant characteristic of dramatic interaction in any situation where morality can be merchandized in the trappings of rational organization.*

The "can be" aspect of the behavior relates to the willingness of the audience to become a partner in the act of impression management. And such a partnership may be expected on any occasion where the *context* of the event is more important than its *content*. The audience is neither gulled nor mystified: the ingratiating response with which it reinforces the performance is a fair exchange for the perpetuation of cherished illusions.

Illustrations of this hypothesis may be found in all kinds of organizations concerned with activity which is essentially moral—i.e., activity which in some way defines the character of the participants. Granting that there are many people sincerely interested in self-improvement or community improvement, it must also be acknowledged that there are also many who are interested in appearing to be interested.

Thus, to attend a Mental Health function is to identify oneself as the kind of person who attends such functions. The same is true of attending church, the symphony, a Legion convention, or a John Birch Society meeting. When the opera opens in Pangloss, the demand for rental of undertaker's limousines exceeds the supply; yet some of the same gentlemen who provide an impeccable context for their ladies' grand entrance can be observed sleeping serenely through the most content-full arias, their dutiful applause cued-in by wifely nudges.

The contention that context is more important than content can be supported by inferences drawn from post-performance audience comments. The principal address at an agency educational function is rarely evaluated on the basis of what the speaker said, but is generally dismissed as either "tremendously interesting" or "a bit dull." By contrast, the personality of the speaker evokes precise adjectives. He may be described as "dynamic," "sexy," "scholarly," or "cold." In what staff members considered to be one of the Association's most provocative annual meetings, a speaker from the Joint Commission of Mental Health and Mental Illness (a bit worn after a day of meeting the press) delivered an address which challenged the very foundation of the mental health movement. But the audience was unmoved. The consensus of most participants was expressed by a Board member who said: "Too bad he wasn't more dynamic, but we sure got great publicity!" (Field notes).

By and large, an audience will be cooperative for any performance which provides it an image-enhancing context. So long as proper attention has been given to creature comforts and propriety, so long as the import of the occasion is reified by the press, and so long as the attendance is quantitatively impressive, the person who wishes to appear in this particular moral light will accept the proffered package on the basis of its wrappings.

Thus, one may move from agency to agency, from committee meeting to committee meeting, and observe the same script eliciting the same responses. Even the audiences are the same—the obligated, the dedicated, and the status seekers. Over the years, the faces change: the children finally reach college-expense age and the husband's resistance to his wife's "doing something worthwhile"—i.e., working for pay rather than progress—is finally worn down, and a volunteer replacement is needed. Or the business man, having served his apprenticeship in community service, moves to a higher level of decision making and can delegate his previous chores to a junior executive.

But there are always new people to be seduced by the agency imagery—to respond to the structured illusion which promises the most satisfaction for the least effort. By the same token, although it may take longer, the agency will find new idealists to fill the old staff vacancies—people who will perceive the role as offering an opportunity for the realization of an idealized self.

Daniel Boorstin, in *The Image* (1961: 3) maintains:

> Each of us individually provides the market and the demand for the illusions which flood our experiences.. . . We want and believe these illusions because we suffer from extravagant expectations.

The image is an end product of rational organization. In social welfare, it fills the demand for bargain morality. The dramatization of virtue provides the credit card which permits individuals, collectivities, and societies to live beyond their moral means.

THE ENTROPIC RELATIONSHIP

Since all of us are dissemblers, our knowledge of our own discreditable reality leads us to believe that impression management is, at least to some degree, a kindly vice.

In reality, impression management is amoral. The crucial factor is the relationship. Do we view our audiences with respect or contempt? If we recall Goffman's discussion of audience motivation, we recognize that although all impression management is manipulatory, the attempt to increase one's attractiveness to others is not always entirely predicated on personal gain.

Certainly it would be risky to pose a dichotomy of purely altruistic and purely selfish behaviors. But Goffman's first classification, identification, is a basis for interaction in which actors respond out of sympathy, empathy, and respect for their common humanity. In relationships charactertized by identification, the impressions we foster are attempts to win the good opinions of those we admire. And in making the attempt, we tend to become, at least momentarily the ideal self we are trying to project. Thus, through our deference, demeanor and tact, we make interaction possible, pleasant, and sustaining.

When there is gross misrepresentation of reality, interaction sustained for the sake of scene avoidance is questionable. It preserves the status quo, inhibits challenge of the incompetent, conceals dissensus, and precludes the asking of the embarrassing question which can propel a group toward reconsideration of the relevance of old objectives to a changing environment. Confrontation is not a comfortable alternative—but when channels of communication have become hopelessly clogged, the passivity of the scene avoider can contribute to loss of information, loss of organization, and loss of vitality.

Identification and scene avoidance are motivations for tactful responses in the audience-actor repertoire designed to support others or spare them embarrassment. But interaction which is characterized by ingratiation is based on contempt. It is an entropic process which degrades, dehumanizes, and finally destroys the integrity of the personality, the group, and the society. If communicative integration is the essential integration which cuts through all others, it is this which ingratiation most surely destroys.

180

The process demeans both the ingratiator and the ingratiated. The ingratiating student, laughing with concealed insincerity at an instructor's feeble humor, contributes to the perpetuation of a mediocre performance. The ingratiating congregation, rewarding the Jesus-loves-me sermon, contributes to the timidity of the clergyman with a social conscience. And the Uncle Tom, by contributing to the white man's self deception, must bear some of the guilt for diminishing the humanity of both his own race and the white man's. Ingratiation amplifies deviance.

But what is the ultimate outcome? What happens to the makers and the made? If we may judge from current and historical examples, there are two possibilities. In the first, the boldness of the manipulator increases the credibility gap to the point where someone deflates the bloated image and the illusion is destroyed. Ralph Nader exposed the naked reality of the automobile manufacturer's attitude toward public safety. Fred Friendly revealed the communicative manipulations of a medium of information. Citizen Doe, embracing medicare, shattered the self-deception of the American Medical Association. And race riots have destroyed the illusion that an anti-poverty payoff can bring contentment to the ghetto.

The Coerced Redefinition

When an organization is incapable of responding to the demands for a new reality, it must yield to a new organization. One of the most interesting examples of this is the Protestant Reformation. Long before Luther, there were other monks who found the imagery of the Church unacceptable. But they wrote their findings in scholarly Latin, and their protests were lodged with superiors who were well able to conceal the destructive information. However, in "The Ink-Blot on the Wartburg Wall," Donald Elder (1966: 8) suggests that much of Luther's effectiveness was the result of the fifteenth century intersection of technology and theology. The rapid spread of Luther's ideas was made posssible by the invention of moveable type. Thus, Luther's writings, printed in the language of the people, became the first best sellers—a real breakthrough in the information barrier which had protected the status quo. It should also be noted that Protestantism discarded the norm of most-least which had enabled people to delegate their good works through the purchase of indulgences. Substituted in its stead was the rigorous worldly asceticism of Calvinism.

Thus, revolt against imagery and subsequent reform is one outcome. However, where reform was the initial objective of an organization, the imagery results in ultimate goal displacement. In relation to Mental Health, we originally suggested that the staff perceived image manipulation as a means of achieving goals in a hostile environment; and that this strategy was viewed as a *temporary measure* designed to mobilize resources. The goal of escalating action was not abandoned—only deferred.

We have attempted to show that such a strategy is based on a false premise, and thus it becomes a self-fulfilling prophecy. The agency which promises the most-least must actually attempt to provide the most satisfaction for the least effort. By gearing its operation to the mass expectation of pseudo-involvement, it manufactures pseudo events for pseudo community leaders, thus decreasing the opportunities for those individuals who want real involvement. Moreover, by concealing destructive information concerning a worthless program, *it creates an image which it dares not destroy.*

Therefore, to manufacture an image is not only to build a better mousetrap—but to take up residence there. And when the rewards for such residence are great, the desire to escape is continuously eroded.

The Question

Is the Pangloss Mental Health Association an action group or a diversionary movement? Certainly one can say that some of its programs divert action from professed goals of improved care and treatment for mental patients. For example, in the Christmas project, the mind boggles in contemplating what all that money and all that energy could accomplish. More research, perhaps. Or better yet—what the patients really need for Christmas—a good psychiatrist!

Would the community buy it? Certainly. Even without the Association or the United Fund. All it would require would be a group of dedicated volunteers . . .

somebody to answer the telephone . . .

and a good P.R. man . . . .

NOTES
ON METHODOLOGY

As an end-point in analysis, the dramaturgical framework is a research tool with infinite possibilities and definite limitations. It provides a means of separating the illusion from the underlying reality, and has a special applicability to any organization which is in a position to substitute packaging for product—or context for content. It is a heuristic device for providing the hypotheses which can be tested by conventional statistical methods; and it avoids the tautologies of functionalism. It also appears to offer exciting potential in the area of comparative studies.

The method is frankly subjective; and certainly in my situation, my participation influenced the action. Moreover, this method is one which requires some dissembling on the part of the sociologist. One may be welcomed to study an organization's public relations techniques—but to suggest an interest in manipulative devices is to cool the hospitable response.

The method also presents difficulties in confining data to manageable proportions—and yet, in apologizing for too great a scope, I regret those important events which had to be eliminated in respect for the reader's endurance.

While dramaturgical analysis provides the means for examining an organization's ability to foster effectively an impression of effectiveness, it has limitations as a criterion for ineffectiveness. In the absence of rigorous procedures for the evaluation of what audiences actually gain from the performances, the observer can only speculate.

In a cybernated society, this framework provides important insights into the communicative acts by which mass society can be "managed." If, as Donald Michael (1965: 156-166) suggests, information technology increases "major psychological problems arising from the depersonalization of relationships within management and the greater distance between people," this kind of painful, illusion-destroying inquiry is necessary. Moreover, as service occupations increasingly replace production work, it becomes doubly important that we understand those mechanisms of information control which can be contrived by any organization dealing in intangibles.

Supplemented by attitude research and comparative studies, the dramaturgical approach could be utilized to identify areas of organizational drift toward diversion of resources and action. Certainly it is replicable. Goffman's framework is so clearly elucidated that replication is possible for almost any reasonably astute observer.

We believe that our initial assumptions, (1) that the PMHA is not unique; and (2) that voluntarism is the essence of community, are valid. But we suggest that verification through comparative studies might provide important additional data on the nature of alienation. There are questions which need exploration. Does the mixture of paid staff and volunteers necessarily create dissonance? Are all-volunteer organizations more, or less, effective than an organizational mix?

The method is also particularly valuable for delineating different types of relationships, and it points a need for further study. In spite of our vaunted objectivity, we in sociology have been prone to describe primary relations as giving deep satisfaction, and secondary relations as coldly instrumental. This nostalgia for Gemeinschaft tends to obscure an important existential relationship. In *The Secular City*, Harvey Cox (1965: 48-49) proposes that urbanization provides the opportunity for "enjoyable I-You relationships" (as contrasted with the I-Thou or I-it) which can be "decidedly human even though they remain somewhat distant." They are essentially open, warmly impersonal relationships based on role-capacity respect rather than the pseudo-Gemeinschaft of the personality merchandisers. Cox proposes an I-You theology. I suggest that the many such relationships—which appear to be an innovation of urban man—deserve serious attention from sociologists.

The New Empiricism is a time-consuming type of research. Essences can only be discovered in a longitudinal study. And yet, my own experience has convinced me that such a time expenditure may be an excellent investment. Maurice Stein (1966) has suggested that all sociologists (like anthropologists) should be required to spend a year of field study in which they subjectively experience the role of the participant in an organization or movement in opposition to the status quo. Even we—or perhaps, especially we—cherish our illusions. The view from the inside is different.

–E.S.

NOTES
AND REFERENCES

NOTES

2 THE COMMUNITY CONTEXT

1. _____ County Association for Mental Health Board Manual, Constitution and By-Laws.
2. _____ County Association for Mental Health Pamphlet.
3. Ibid.

3 DEFINITIONAL DISCREPANCIES

1. Paresis is a psychiatric disorder characterized by mental and physical symptoms, caused by syphilis of the central nervous system. See Hinsie and Shatzky, 1940.

2. The Korsakoff psychosis may be caused by a variety of agents, but it is frequently associated with alcoholism (Hinsie and Shatzky, 1940).

3. Millerism refers to the teachings of William Miller, a preacher who prophesized that the end of the world and the second coming of Christ would occur in 1843.

4. The Mental Health Association survey was a non-random, disproportionately middle class sample of 7,500 people, conducted by 1,500 volunteer interviewers among their neighbors in "Pangloss," 1960.

4 THE FACADE OF FORMAL ORGANIZATION

1. For a brief summary of Weber's discussion, see Parsons, 1958.

9 SYMBIOTIC COOPERATION

1. —————— County Association for Mental Health Board Manual Section: State Association.
2. Field notes: interview with United Fund representative.
3. Ibid.
4. Television editorial, October 7, 1966. Based on United Fund publicity.
5. Information and Consultation Service "served" four hundred clients in 1963 (this includes telephone inquiries). The rehabilitation center served seventeen residents.

11 THE ALIENATION OF STAFF

1. Since neither of these employees was socialized to the performance, their reasons for leaving were not considered relevant to the study.

2. It was during this two-year period that the two staff members who did not complete the training period were hired. Thus neither can be said to have filled the staff roles.

REFERENCES _____

BABCHUK, NICHOLAS, and JOHN N. EDWARDS (1965) "Voluntary Associations and the Integration Hypothesis." *Sociological Inquiry* (Spring): 150.

BEERS, C.W. (1921) A Mind That Found Itself. Garden City, N.Y.: Doubleday.

BLUMER, H. (1951) "Collective Behavior." In A.M. Lee (ed.) Principles of Sociology. New York: Barnes & Noble.

BOORSTIN, DANIEL (1961) The Image. New York: Harper & Row.

BREHM, J.W., and A.R. COHEN (1962) Explorations in Cognitive Dissonance. New York: John Wiley.

BROOM, LEONARD, and PHILIP SELZNICK (1963) Sociology (Third ed.). New York: Harper & Row.

BRUYN, SEVERYN T. (1966) "The New Empiricists: Phenomenologists Observers." Paper presented at the American Sociological Association Annual Meeting, Miami Beach, Florida.

CARTER, RICHARD (1961) The Gentle Legions. Garden City, N.Y.: Doubleday.

Central Region Mental Health Planning Committee (1965) Final Report (November).

COX, HARVEY (1965) The Secular City. New York: Macmillan.

DAVIS, KINGSLEY (1938) "Mental Hygiene and the Class Structure." Psychiatry 1 (January): 55-65.

DE TOCQUEVILLE, ALEXIS (1862) Democracy in America. Cambridge: Sever & Francis.

DEUTSCH, ALFRED (1949) The Mentally Ill in America. New York: Columbia University Press.

ELDER, DONALD (1966) "The Ink-Blot on the Wartburg Wall." Unpublished manuscript.

ETZIONI, AMITAI (1968) The Active Society. New York: Free Press.

——— (1964) Modern Organizations, Foundations of Modern Sociology Series. Englewood Cliffs. N.J.: Prentice-Hall.

FARBEROW, NORMAN L., and EDWIN S. SCHNEIDMAN (1961) The Cry for Help. New York: McGraw-Hill.

FESTINGER, LEON (1957) A Theory of Cognitive Dissonance. Stanford: Stanford University Press.

GLASSER, WILLIAM (1965) "Reality Therapy." Saturday Review of Literature (March 6) 54-55.

190

GOFFMAN, ERVING (1962) Asylums. New York: Doubleday.

—— (1952) "On Cooling the Mark Out." Psychiatry 15 (Nov.):465.

—— (1961) Encounters. Indianapolis: Bobbs-Merrill.

—— (1955) "On Face Work." Psychiatry 18: 213-231.

—— (1959) The Presentation of Self in Everyday Life. Garden City, N.Y.: Doubleday.

—— (1963) Stigma. Englewood Cliffs, N.J.: Prentice-Hall.

GURSSLIN, ORVILLE R., RAYMOND G. HUNT, and JACK L. ROACH (1959-60) "Social Class and the Mental Health Movement." Social Problems 7 (Winter): 210-218.

HINSIE, LELAND E., and JACOB SHATZKY (1940) Psychiatric Dictionary. New York: Oxford University Press.

HOFFER, ERIC (1951) The True Believer. New York: Mentor.

HOMANS, GEORGE (1950) The Human Group. New York: Harcourt, Brace & World.

HUGHES, EVERETT (1964) "Good People and Dirty Work." In Howard Becker (ed.) The Other Side. New York: Free Press of Glencoe.

Joint Commission on Mental Illness and Mental Health (1961) Action for Mental Health (Final Report). New York: Basic Books.

JONES, E.E. (1964) Ingratiation. New York: Appleton-Century-Crofts.

KATZ, DANIEL, and ROBERT KAHN (1966) The Social Psychology of Organizations. New York: John Wiley.

KOMAROVSKY, MIRRA (1946) "The Voluntary Associations of Urban Dwellers." American Sociological Review 11 (Dec.).

MARTIN, J.B. (1959) The Pane of Glass. New York: Harper & Row.

McLUHAN, MARSHALL (1965) Understanding Media, The Extensions of Man. New York: McGraw-Hill.

MERTON, ROBERT (1957) Social Theory and Social Structure. Glencoe, Ill.: Free Press.

191

MICHAEL, DONALD (1965) "The Problems of Automation." In Edward O. McDonagh and John E. Simpson (eds.) Social Problems: Persistent Challenges. New York: Holt, Rinehart & Winston.

NUNNALLY, J.C., Jr. (1961) Popular Conceptions of Mental Health. New York: Holt, Rinehart & Winston.

PARSONS, TALCOTT (1951) The Social System. Glencoe, Ill.: Free Press.

——— (1958) The Structure of Social Action. Glencoe, Ill.: Free Press.

RIESMAN, DAVID (1954) Individualism Reconsidered and Other Essays. Glencoe, Ill.: Free Press.

ROPER, ELMO (1950) "People's Attitudes Concerning Mental Health: A Study Made in the City of Louisville, September, 1950."

SCHEFF, THOMAS (1966) Being Mentally Ill. Chicago: Aldine.

SILLS, DAVID (1957) The Volunteers. Glencoe, Ill.: Free Press.

SELZNICK, PHILIP (1943) "An Approach to a Theory of Bureaucracy." American Sociological Review 8: 49.

STEIN, MAURICE (1966) "Eros and Sociology." Paper presented at the American Sociological Association Annual Meeting. Miami Beach, Florida.

STENGEL, EDWIN (1964) Suicide and Attempted Suicide. Baltimore: Penguin.

SZASZ, T. S. (1960) "The Myth of Mental Illness." American Psychologist 15 (February): 113-118.

TANNENBAUM, FRANK (1938) Crime and the Community. Boston: Ginn.

WILLIAMS, CLIFFORD L. (1950) "A History of Mental Hospitals." Unpublished manuscript.

DATE DUE

GAYLORD   PRINTED IN U.S.A.